HYPER-CALVINISM

TOBIAS CRISP

THE EMERGENCE OF
HYPER-CALVINISM
IN ENGLISH NONCONFORMITY
1689-1765

PETER TOON

WIPF & STOCK · Eugene, Oregon

Wipf and Stock Publishers
199 W 8th Ave, Suite 3
Eugene, OR 97401

The Emergence of Hyper - Calvinism in English
Nonconformity 1689 - 1765
By Toon, Peter and Packer, J. I.
Copyright©1967 by Toon, Peter
ISBN 13: 978-1-60899-688-9
Publication date 02/01/2011
Previously published by The Olive Tree, 1967

CONTENTS

ACKNOWLEDGEMENTS

PREFACE BY THE REV. DR. J. I. PACKER, LATIMER HOUSE, OXFORD

PART I
THE BACKGROUND

I. Calvin and Calvinism 11
II. The Augustan Age 31

PART II
HIGH CALVINISM BECOMES HYPER-CALVINISM

III. Antinomianism and High Calvinism 49
IV. No Offers of Grace 70

PART III
THE PROPAGATION OF HYPER-CALVINISM

V. Three Theologians 93
VI. God, His Decrees and Covenants 104
VII. Man, his Sin and his Salvation 119

PART IV
CONCLUSION

VIII. A Definition of Hyper-Calvinism 143
APPENDIX
    I. The Diary of Joseph Hussey 153
    II. The Doctrinal Basis of the King's Head Society 154
BIBLIOGRAPHY 158
INDEX 169

ACKNOWLEDGEMENTS

I AM grateful to many people for their help but I would like especially to mention the following: the Rev. Dr. G. F. Nuttall, Rev. R. Thomas, Rev. E. F. Clipsham, Mr. I. Sellers, Mr. P. Helm, Mr. L. F. Lupton, and Mr. L. Thorpe. The Rev. Dr. J. I. Packer and the Rev. Dr. I. Breward gave me permission to quote from their theses.

Dr. Williams's Library, The Evangelical Library, New College Library (London), New College Library (Edinburgh), the Gospel Standard Library (Brighton), and the Selby Branch of the West Riding County Library gave me excellent service.

PETER TOON.

Durham.
September, 1967.

ABBREVIATIONS.

B.Q. = "Baptist Quarterly".
C.H. = "Church History".
D.N.B. = "Dictionary of National Biography".
E.Q. = "Evangelical Quarterly".
J.E.H. = "Journal of Ecclesiastical History".
J.Th.S. = "Journal of Theological Studies".
T.C.H.S. = "Transactions of the Congregational Historical Society".

PREFACE

THIS book is a first attempt to fill a long-standing gap—not, unhappily, the only one—in the story of English "Calvinism". Partly, no doubt, because few in recent years have thought of the Reformed faith as more than an outmoded oddity, the study of its history from the first Elizabeth to the second has been neglected. Hence the most vehement adherents of "the Reformed position" to-day are often unaware of the different sorts of "Reformed position" that this country has seen. This is not, of course, to deny the basic continuity of the English Reformed tradition, any more than it is to endorse all the attempts to detect differences that individual scholars have made. But it is to point out that those who profess the Reformed faith should know that at certain points their profession may mean more than one thing.

With its stress on the rationality of God and man, and therefore of revelation and of true Christian life and worship, Calvinism has great intellectual strength—a strength that easily becomes weakness, when dry intellectualism and rationalism take over. By the end of the seventeenth century, the crippling touch of rationalism was apparent within the Puritan tradition: a delusive reliance on natural theology, the taproot of Latitudinarianism and Deism among Anglicans, was starting to produce Unitarianism among Dissenters, as it had already produced the neo-legalism of Baxter (not to mention the Carolines, and the Arminians in Holland), to whom the Gospel was a new law. All these tendencies struck, in one way or another, at the free sovereignty of God, which to Calvinists is of the essence of His glory. Not surprisingly, therefore, the eighteenth century saw a reaction against such trends, a reaction which saw itself as a rediscovery of the true line of Reformed development. But, in an increasingly rationalistic age, the reaction itself was as rationalistic, within the Reformed supernaturalistic frame, as the movements away from that frame had been. In its teaching about man, sin and grace (always the staple themes of Reformed interest), this reaction fairly ran the thought of God's free sovereignty to death. It earned itself the name, "Hyper-Calvinism". This is the development whose rise and fall Mr. Toon traces in the following pages. The story is a cautionary tale with timely lessons for those who seek a revival of Reformed Christianity to-day.

Latimer House, Oxford.   J. I. PACKER.
July, 1967.

PART ONE

THE BACKGROUND

CHAPTER I

CALVIN AND CALVINISM

Synopsis: 1. Authentic Calvinism, a balanced theology. 2. Beza and Calvinism. 3. Perkins and Calvinism. 4. Three modifications of High Calvinism: (*a*) Arminianism, (*b*) Federal Theology, (*c*) Amyraldism. 5. Orthodox Puritanism and Calvinism. 6. Doctrinal Antinomianism.

Those who called themselves "Calvinists" in the period which we are to study did not derive their doctrines solely from John Calvin. When the Toleration Act was passed in England in 1689, Calvin had been dead for over one hundred years and a host of theologians, meeting in Synods and individually writing books, had added much to what Calvin had originally written. It was from parts of this long tradition of Reformed teaching that the "Calvinists" of the eighteenth century received the basic materials with which to make their own brand of Calvinism. In this chapter it is our task to survey rapidly the major developments of Calvinism from the death of Calvin in 1564 until the year 1689, and we shall make particular reference to those which took place within, or affected, English theology. Since we are only concerned with those doctrines which describe the redemption and restoration of man, we shall not notice developments in the doctrines of Church polity or the relationship of Church and State.

AUTHENTIC CALVINISM. A BALANCED THEOLOGY

John Calvin learned much of his theology from the writings of the reformers who began their work before he entered Geneva, such men as Martin Luther, Ulrich Zwingli, Martin Bucer and Philip Melanchthon. He also found much to stimulate and guide his thinking in the books of the great bishop of North Africa, Augustine of Hippo. Yet in Calvin's own books, especially in the Biblical commentaries and the *Institutes*, we see the great expositor at work, always seeking, in his clear style, to maintain a balanced exegesis and to pay full regard to both the doctrines of divine sovereignty in human salvation and human responsibility to obey God at all times. It is true that at times he seemed to develop to a logical conclusion ideas which are only suggested in Scripture (*e.g.* his doctrine of double predestination which Bullinger of Zurich did not share), but this is the exception rather than the rule. His commentaries are being republished today because laymen, students and ministers now recognise that they contain sound learning and a thoroughly Biblical theology, all of which is explained in a simple and profound manner.

Many efforts have been made to try to state the central, dominating doctrine of his theological system. Of these, the most popular suggestion, since Alexandre Schweizer and Ferdinand Christian first made it in the 1840s, has been that of predestination.[1] Perhaps it is impossible to state what was the central doctrine of his system. As he built the *Institutes* around the pattern found in the Apostles' Creed, it is legitimate to assume that he believed that all the major doctrines of the Christian faith, as contained in that Creed, had to be maintained in careful balance. In the exciting years of the mid-sixteenth century his theology, commonly called "Calvinism", was well fitted to capture the hearts and minds of thousands in Europe. And it did just this.

After the death of Calvin there was a growing preoccupation with Aristotelian metaphysics. (The Aristotelianism of the earlier years of the Reformation had been greatly modified by the humanist tradition and had only involved logic and rhetoric.) This use of Aristotelianism received an impetus in the controversies which soon developed amongst Protestants. The Christological issue within Lutheranism, the predestinarian problems within the Reformed tradition and the conflict over Christ's presence in the Lord's Supper, all had the consequence of intensifying the tendency to express truth through precise definition and the drawing of fine distinctions. So Protestants began to do what the medieval schoolmen had done and this use of scholastic method was intensified by the challenge produced by a renewed Roman Catholicism, which sought to find the weaknesses of the Protestant position.[2] We may see the effects of this growing preoccupation with Aristotelianism by considering four Protestant doctrines: predestination, original sin, atonement and justification. In looking at them we shall make special reference to the influence of Theodore Beza since he was the successor of Calvin at Geneva from where he exerted a wide influence.

BEZA AND CALVINISM

Predestination. Though Calvin had taught a doctrine of predestination which included a decree of election and a decree of reprobation, he had also warned against speculation into these mysteries. Not all of his disciples seem to have heeded this advice. Beza placed the doctrine of predestination under the doctrine of God and His providence (where Aquinas had discussed it), and also advocated, what was later called, "supralapsarianism".[3] That is, he saw the following order in the eternal decrees of God. First, the decree to manifest justice and mercy in the salvation of some human beings and the rejection of others. Secondly, the decree to create the human race, and thirdly, the decree to permit the sin of Adam. (Other followers of Calvin placed the decree to create mankind before the decree of election and reprobation. This order of the decrees was termed "sublapsarianism" or "infralapsarianism".) The very idea of speculating about the processes of God's mind was repugnant to Calvin. In his treatise, *Concerning the Eternal Predestination of God*, he wrote:

But it is right to treat this whole question (of God permitting the fall of man) sparingly, not because it is abstruse and hidden in the inner recesses of the sanctuary of God, but because an idle curiosity is not to be indulged. . . . I much approve what Augustine has to say in the *De Genesi ad Litteram*, where he subjects all things to the fear and reverence of God. But the other part, showing that God chose out of the condemned race of Adam those whom He pleased and reprobated whom He willed, is much more fitting for the exercise of faith and so yields greater profit. Hence, I emphasise more willingly this doctrine which deals with the corruption and guilt of human nature, since it seems to me not only more conducive to piety but also more theological.[4]

Two famous English Puritans who adopted supralapsarianism were William Perkins and William Twisse. Not only did

Perkins believe that this logical presentation of predestination was Biblical but, betraying the effects of the scholastic concept of reason, he felt obliged to show how it agreed "with the grounds of common reason, which may be obtained by the light of reason". In the "epistle to the reader" in his book, *A Christian and Plaine Treatise . . . of Predestination*, Perkins gave a list of ten points of "common reason" which he thought agreed with the Biblical teaching.

Original Sin. As we have seen in the quotation given above, Calvin emphasised the transmission of a depraved moral nature from one generation to the next, and from parents to children; yet he gave little prominence to the doctrine that God imputed to every descendant of Adam the guilt of Adam's first sin. In the chapters of the *Institutes* in which he expounded the doctrine of original sin his interest is concentrated in the possession by each human being of a depraved nature.

> We see that the impurity of parents is transmitted to their children, so that all, without exception, are originally depraved. The commencement of this depravity will not be found until we ascend to the first parent of all as the fountain head. We must, therefore, hold it for certain that, in regard to human nature, Adam was not merely a progenitor, but, as it were, a root, and that accordingly, by his corruption, the whole human race was deservedly vitiated.[5]

Two reasons are usually suggested to explain Calvin's apparent lack of interest in the doctrine of the imputation of Adam's sin, which doctrine in later years was accepted by the majority of Reformed divines. First, it is possible that he did not regard it as important. Secondly, since some of his Roman Catholic opponents accepted the doctrine, it is suggested that he had no need to stress it.[6] There would seem to be more truth in the first reason than the second since Calvin did emphasise some doctrines which he held in common with the Roman Catholic Church. The systematic exposition of the doctrine of the imputation of Adam's sin is to be traced to Beza and it was through his influence that it was quickly accepted and taught as a standard doctrine of the Reformed faith.

Atonement. There is no systematic exposition in Calvin's writings of the doctrine that Christ died only for the elect. In his comments on 1 John 2. 2, he expressed his agreement with the scholastic expression that "Christ suffered sufficiently for the whole world but effectively only for the elect". And in his *Acta Synodi Tridentinae: Cum Antidoto*, he passed by, quite deliberately, and without comments, an explicit declaration that Christ died for all men. It is perhaps fair to state that the extent of the atonement does not seem to have been a problem which agitated the mind of Calvin. Only in later discussions of election and the efficacy of Christ's death did the question, as to the precise extent of the atonement, arise. Beza adopted the view that Christ died only for the elect and maintained this doctrine in his controversial writings against the Lutherans.[7] It soon became a prominent article of the Reformed faith and was championed in England by Perkins. Concerning the latter's view of Christ's death, Ian Breward has written that "his interpretation of the atonement suggests that he saw it in the light of the decree (of election) rather than *vice versa*".[8] Certainly Calvin cannot be accused of reading the doctrine of election into the doctrine of the atonement.

Justification. Since he had the Roman Catholic doctrine of justification in mind, Calvin frequently explained that justification is not the same as regeneration; justification is an act of God in which He declares, through Christ's redeeming work, that a sinner is forgiven. Sometimes Calvin spoke of justification not merely as forgiveness of sin but also as acceptance through Christ's righteousness with God, although this latter idea is not so prominent as the former in his writings. Certainly he never made a distinction, as did later Reformed divines, between the active and passive righteousness of Christ. "It was perhaps," wrote Dr. Cunningham, "more in accordance with the cautious and reverential spirit in which he usually conducted his investigations into divine things to abstain from any minute and definite statements regarding it."[9] The origin of the distinction between the active and passive righteousness of Christ is probably to be traced to the militant

Lutheran, Flavius Illyricus, and the Danish theologian, Nicolaus Hemmingius.[10] Beza adopted this distinction and taught that justification consists not only in the forgiveness of sins through Christ's death, but also the imputation of the righteousness of Christ, founded upon His active obedience to the law of God.[11] This doctrine became the orthodox Reformed view.

PERKINS AND CALVINISM

Reference has already been made to the famous Cambridge theologian, William Perkins, whose writings and preaching exerted such a great influence upon English Puritanism. His theological thought provides a good example of the changes taking place in Reformed theology at the end of the sixteenth century. "He was more than a theological thermometer whose popularisations registered the current atmosphere, but he further developed changes of emphasis already present in Reformed theology."[12] Two of these changes of emphasis, to which as yet we have not made any reference, were in the relationship of faith to Christ and Scripture and in the grounds of Christian assurance.

In his earliest writings Perkins frequently defined faith with reference to a direct relationship to Christ. Later he came to lay more emphasis upon the relationship of faith to the words of God in Holy Scripture. He defined faith as "a gift of God whereby we give assent or credence to God's Word". He held that "it is all one to say the saving promise and Christ promised" is the object of faith.[13] The earlier reformers, Luther and Calvin, had believed that the conjunction of Word and Spirit made the Scriptures normative through the way in which they created and nourished faith. As the Bible came to be regarded as a book of metaphysical knowledge concentration upon what it *directly* said assumed a greater role. The efficacy of Scripture rested no more on the work of the Spirit, but upon the identification of the text and the Spirit, through a conception of the Bible as verbally inspired and inerrant. The Bible was thus seen as a book of delivered truth; theology was the orderly statement of truth and truth became identical with propositional statement. This identification is seen very clearly in the five "points" of the Remonstrants and in the five "counter-points" of the High Calvinists at the Synod of Dort in 1619. Whilst Luther and Calvin had moved from the authority of the Bible to the inerrancy of the text, later Reformed teachers moved in the reverse direction.[14] The battle with Roman Catholicism over the authority of the Bible also caused the Protestants to defend the Bible as the recorded document of the very words of God Himself. Perkins' position was, as it were, a half-way point between Calvin and the High Calvinists who attended the Synod of Dort.

One of the chief characteristics of Puritanism was its great interest in the doctrine of the assurance of eternal salvation and in the related problems of conscience. The reason for this absorbing interest may perhaps be traced to two sources. First, many ordinary people had been thrown into spiritual chaos by the sweeping changes made in the parish church in regard to the services of worship and the religious observances; these people needed counsel and help. Secondly, the Englishman is pragmatic by nature and thus he tends to be most concerned with that which seems to him most useful and practical; the Puritans concerned themselves with what they considered to be the most important question of all. In the words of Perkins this was, "How may a man know whether he be a child of God or no?" A comparison of the teaching of Calvin and Perkins on assurance reveals that the latter gave a much more affirmative place with regard to the testimony of good works to election than did Calvin. In *A Case of Conscience, the greatest that ever was: How a Man may know whether he be a Child of God or No* (1592), Perkins wrote:

This is one of the chiefest uses of good works that by them, not as by cause, as by effects of predestination and faith, both we and also our neighbours are certified of our election and salvation too.[15]

Calvin preferred to lay emphasis on personal faith in Christ and union to Him as well as on God's sanctifying gifts to His people, since "works, when estimated by themselves, no less (prove) the divine displeasure by their imperfection, than his good-will by their incipient purity".[16]

As Basil Hall has recently put it: "It is arguable that with the political and theological changes, which came after Calvin's death, within the framework of the national churches of the Reformation, and the bitter struggle between Catholic and Protestant in Europe, Calvinism was bound to change. This is true but it is not the same thing as to say that the changes were inevitable and right in the direction they took".[17] Indeed, as perhaps the latter part of this study will reveal, the later history of Calvinist thought would seem to suggest that some of the changes in, and additions to, Calvin's theology were not the right ones. However, the Biblical humanism of Calvin is to be preferred to the logical orthodoxy of much of the later Reformed teaching.

Three Modifications of High Calvinism

Having briefly described the growth of a rigid form of Calvinism which we shall call "High Calvinism", we shall now describe three important theological systems whose origins and compilation were conditioned by some form of reaction or protest against High Calvinism. The three are Arminianism, Federal Theology and Amyraldism.

Arminianism. The first major revolt against High Calvinism is associated with the name of James Arminius who became professor of theology at Leyden in 1603. Carl Bangs writes of Arminius that he "articulates a position which he feels to be a valid reformed theology of grace in harmony with the earliest sentiments of the Reformed churches in Switzerland and Holland".[18] But the term "Arminianism" has been given to many varying theological systems which bear some similarity to the thought of Arminius and which are opposed to the basic dogmas of High Calvinism.

The theological problem which caused Arminius to doubt the Bezan doctrine of grace was the relation of supralapsarian predestination to human freedom and responsibility. In his definitive *Declaration of Sentiments* (1608), he insisted that predestination must be understood as "in Christ" rather than being referred to the inscrutable and secret counsel of

God. He outlined his own view of predestination in four decrees.

The first absolute decree of God concerning the salvation of sinful men is that by which he decreed to appoint his Son, Jesus Christ, for a Mediator, Redeemer, Saviour, Priest and King who might destroy sin in his death, might by his obedience obtain the salvation which had been lost and might communicate it by his own virtue.

The second decree extends the scope of the "absolute decree" to include all those who "repent and believe" in Christ. The third decree describes the administration of "sufficient and efficient" means necessary for the repentance and faith of those who believe. It is in terms of the fourth decree that Arminius is best known.

To these succeeds the fourth decree by which God decreed to save and damn certain particular persons. This decree has its foundation in the foreknowledge of God by which he knew from all eternity those individuals who would, through his preventing grace, believe, and through his subsequent grace, persevere, according to the before mentioned administration of those means which are proper and suitable for conversion and faith; and by which foreknowledge he likewise knew those who would not believe and persevere . . . .[19]

Though he gave a Christological interpretation to predestination, Arminius differed from both Calvin and Beza, who both held that God elected people not on the basis of divine foreknowledge of faith, but merely out of divine, sovereign pleasure. Likewise his doctrine that the will is free to choose or reject salvation was not advocated by Calvin or Beza.

The full theological emphasis of those who accepted and developed the theology of Arminius may be clearly seen in the famous five propositions drawn up by the Remonstrants in Holland. In summarised form they are:

1. Man is never so completely corrupted by sin that he cannot savingly believe the Gospel when it is put before him: nor

2. Is he ever so completely controlled by God that he cannot reject it.

3. God's election of those who shall be saved is prompted by His foreseeing that they will believe of their own accord.

4. Christ's death did not ensure the salvation of anyone, for it did not secure the gift of faith to anyone; what it did was to create a possibility of salvation for all who believe.
5. It rests with believers to keep themselves in a state of grace by keeping up their faith; those who fail here fall away and are lost.

These doctrines were not new. Most of them had been the subjects of discussion in Cambridge and London in the 1590s.[20] Yet the troubles which led to, and surrounded, the Synod of Dort helped to make them widely known.[21] In England they were favoured by the High Church party in the seventeenth century and after the Restoration by the majority of Anglicans. After 1689 a growing number of Nonconformists also adopted Arminianism.

Federal Theology. To class Federal Theology with Arminianism as some form of protest against, or, at least, a part-escape from, the rigidity of certain scholastic developments of late sixteenth and early seventeenth-century Reformed theology may surprise those whose view of the development of Calvinist theology is conditioned by the reading of the books of the well-known American federal theologians, Charles Hodge and Benjamin Warfield. Yet this is what it was. The backbone of Federal Theology is the belief that God's relationships with men are always through and by means of covenants. The "covenant of works" was the term used to describe the covenant which, it was believed, God made with Adam as the representative of the whole human race, demanding from him perfect obedience, and promising to him immortality as a reward. The term "covenant of grace" (sometimes "covenant of redemption") was used to describe the agreement of the Holy Trinity to save the elect by providing a Saviour and Advocate for them.

Calvin only spoke of the one covenant, the covenant of grace, and his emphasis was upon its historical manifestation in history: "God has never made any other covenant than that He made formerly with Abraham and at length confirmed by the hand of Moses".[22] He never mentioned a covenant made with Adam. Zwingli and Bullinger also made use of the doctrine of the covenant. Their primary emphasis was upon the moral responsibility of men within the covenant to live for God's glory, but they also made use of it as a defence of infant baptism. The same ethical emphasis is found in William Tyndale's final edition of his *New Testament* (1534), and this had a wide influence in England.[23]

The doctrine of the "covenant of works" seems to have had its origin in the application of the scholastic doctrine of the *lex naturae* to the story of the perfect Adam in the Garden of Eden. Signs of systematisation of the early Reformed doctrine of the covenant of grace can be discerned in the distinction by Musculus between a general covenant with all men and a special covenant concluded with Abraham. Ursinus also distinguished between a covenant of nature and a covenant of grace, whilst his Heidelberg colleague, Olevianus, seems to have been the first to use the expression, "covenant of works", though he linked it with the Mosaic covenant only. William Perkins also referred to the Mosaic covenant as a "covenant of works".[24]

In 1594, Franz Gomarus spoke of a "natural covenant" made with Adam and all men, and a "supernatural covenant" made with the elect. Yet Robert Rollock, a Scotsman, in his *Questiones et responsiones* (1595), seems to have been the first to refer to a "covenant of works" made with Adam in his innocency.[25] It is difficult to ascertain why it was that Federal Theology became popular in the 1590s. The effort to show that even elect men have a moral responsibility to God, the common tendency to schematise Protestant theology, the desire to present a plan of salvation which offered no chinks for Roman Catholic controversialist lances and the growing tendency in European thought to change social relationships from status to contract, all played their part.

In order to avoid extreme predestinarianism, William Ames dichotomised the covenant of grace into the covenant of redemption (the agreement of the Trinity to save the elect) and the covenant of grace (the offer of grace in the Gospel to those who repent and believe). Samuel Rutherford, David Dickson and Richard Baxter, amongst others, adopted this distinction, although in the latter part of the seventeenth century it was generally only made use of by those who followed in the theological tradition of R. Baxter.

The complete Federal Theology of the early seventeenth century combined various strands of Reformation thought and made these into a systematic whole through the use of Ramist logic and method. Though it did stimulate much that was good in the religious life of the English Puritans, the Scottish Covenanters and the New England settlers, it did gradually harden into an arid theological system, just as the theology of Calvin hardened into scholastic Calvinism. In Part III of this study we shall notice some of the effects of this hardening of Federal Theology,[26] as they appeared in English Calvinism.

Amyraldism. John Cameron, a Scotsman, became in 1618, at the request of Duplessis-Mornay, the "Pope of Calvinism", professor of theology at the Protestant Academy of Saumur. His influence on some of his students was such that between them, when they became teachers, they produced a system of theology which has been given such names as "New Methodism", "Salmurianism" and "Amyraldism". Writing about Cameron, Walter Rex states that "he brought to France an antidote to the stultifying rigidity of the post-Dordrecht conservatives; his rethinking of the theological commonplaces set Calvinism on a new path after his death".[27] In fact every important change which occurred in French Calvinism between 1634 and the Revocation can be traced eventually back to him.

The doctrines advocated by Cameron and his students (*e.g.* Moyse Amyraut, Louis Cappel, David Blondel and Jean Daillé) which differed from High Calvinism concerned predestination, Christ's atonement and the psychology of conversion. The double decree of election and reprobation was abandoned and replaced by the decree of election, which was itself placed after the decree of universal redemption. This reversal of the order of the decrees brought the charge of "new method" and the title "New Methodists". In place of limited atonement "hypothetic universalism" was taught. This meant that Christ had died for all men in the sense that the benefits of His death were offered to all who fulfilled the conditions of the Gospel which are repentance and faith. In fact they believed that those who did accept the Gospel were those whom God had chosen in the decree of election. The doctrine of "hypothetic universalism" was set in the context of the dichotomy of the covenant of grace into the covenant of redemption concluded in eternity and the covenant of grace offered in the preaching of the Gospel.

The majority of High Calvinists believed that when God converted a sinner He acted directly upon both the intellect and will of the person concerned. He convinced the mind of His truth and constrained the will to accept His offered grace. Cameron taught that God acted solely on the mind, but because of the inter-relation of mind and will, the will is eventually affected even as the effect follows the cause. This way of describing conversion was meant to soften the harsh idea that the term "irresistible grace" suggests. It made conversion more of an intellectual response to God's truth.

Needless to say the members of the Salmurian school believed that they were recovering the original Reformation emphases and doctrines. The effect of their teaching was felt in seventeenth-century England. In an epistle "To the Associated Ministers of Worcester",[28] Richard Baxter wrote that the doctrine of universal redemption was held by "half the divines of England". Apart from Baxter himself, these included such men as John Preston, William Whateley, John Ball, Nathaniel Culverwell, Richard Vines, Bishop Davenant and Archbishop Ussher. Yet the Salmurian doctrine of the will does not seem to have attracted as much interest in England as the doctrine of universal redemption.

Richard Baxter revised the "New Methodism" of Saumur and produced "Neonomianism", the doctrine that the Gospel is a new law of grace.[29] This moderated Calvinism proved popular amongst Presbyterians after 1662 and amongst both Presbyterians and Congregationalists after 1700.

It is important to note that many of the leading proponents

of Arminianism, Federal Theology and Amyraldism made use of a logical method quite different from the Aristotelian, peripatetic method of Beza and his followers. Arminius defended Ramist logic against the criticisms of Beza in Geneva, and nearly all the exponents of Federal Theology and Amyraldism owed much of their arrangement of material to Ramist principles.

Pierre de la Ramée was a professor in Paris in the middle years of the sixteenth century. He substituted a simple logic for the complicated Aristotelian logic which was taught in the schools of Paris. His new logical method was set out in his famous work, *Dialecticae libri duo*, which had many editions and was translated into many languages. Two of the key words in his system are "dichotomy" and "method". He believed that the way to analyse any of the arts, be that art grammar, dialectic, rhetoric or mathematics, was to use dichotomy. That is, embedded in the nature of things he believed there was an inherent dichotomy. Thus in all definitions of the arts there was dichotomy, as each definition was made up of two parts, each of which subsequently divided into two more parts. The Ramist method of arrangement was to put that which is most general first, and then arrange all subsequent axioms in order, making sure that the more general ones came first and the most obscure last of all. Applying this logic to theology in his *Commentariorum de religione christiana* (1576), he defined theology as "the art of living well", which he divided into "the need for proper faith" and "the actions of faith, man's observance of God's laws".[30]

Numerous theologians in Protestant Europe and in New England arranged their books and encyclopaedias on Ramist lines. Amongst these were Johannes Piscator (1546-1625) Amandus Polanus von Polandsdorf (1561-1610), Johannes Wolleb (1586-1629), Bartholomaus Keckermann (1571-1609) and Johann Heinrich Alsted (1588-1638). Three Englishmen who adopted Ramist principles in Cambridge in the sixteenth century were William Temple, George Downame and Alexander Richardson, although the greatest English Ramist was William Ames whose teaching career was in the early seventeenth century. The latter exerted a great influence in England, New England and in Europe. His most well-known books are the *Medulla Theologiae* and *De Conscientia*.[31]

In the writings of Richardson, Ames and Alsted there is to be found a development of Ramism which was called "technometria" or "technologia". For Ames, at least, this meant integrating ethics and metaphysics into theology so that theology involved both theory and practice. The six basic arts which made up technologia were logic, rhetoric, grammar, physics, mathematics and theology. The basic presupposition of the method was that when God formed the Universe He did it on the basis of a plan which He had in His eternal mind. Thus the tasks of the various arts was to study the created world and discover the basis of each part. And when the findings of each art are put together there will exist a comprehensive world-view and spiritual knowledge. Perry Miller expressed it in the following way: "God created the arts by the method of genesis combining arguments into the patterns of His intention, but man must find the principles of the arts by the method of analysis, discriminating the particulars within the synthesis".[32] No word, it was felt, could describe the thoughts of God, but the "ideas" of the universe in God's decrees were referred to as "archetypal", the principles of these ideas in created objects as "entypal", and, in man's mind as perceived, "ectypal". Technologia thus provided the Puritan with a framework in which, whilst remaining a man of piety and a believer in God's sovereignty and irresistible grace, he could stabilise his intellectual heritage. Yet it demanded great minds to establish and to maintain the synthesis and so there soon occurred a fragmentation of the whole system. Some Puritans clung to the theological dogma and others to the neo-Platonism and the doctrine of innate ideas.

From the same Cambridge Colleges where the English Puritan movement was born there arose a group of thinkers who have become known as the Cambridge Platonists to whom we shall make reference in the next chapter. In Chapter IV we shall see how the doctrine of technologia influenced the Christological doctrine of Thomas Goodwin, and which, in turn, influenced Joseph Hussey in his formulation of an erroneous Christology.

Orthodox Puritanism and Calvinism

The most comprehensive statement of the general Reformed teaching of British seventeenth-century divines is to be found in the *Westminster Confession of Faith* (1647).[33] This document has since become the chief doctrinal standard of Presbyterian churches through the world. Its first nineteen chapters deal with the following topics:

1, Holy Scripture; 2, God and the Holy Trinity; 3, God's Eternal Decree; 4, Creation; 5, Providence; 6, Fall of man, Sin, Punishment; 7, God's covenant with man; 8, Christ the Mediator; 9, Free Will; 10, Effectual Calling; 11, Justification; 12, Adoption; 13, Sanctification; 14, Saving Faith; 15, Repentance unto Life; 16, Good Works; 17, Perseverance of the Saints; 18, Assurance of Grace and Salvation; 19, The Law of God.

A careful reading of these chapters reveals that the doctrines of the *Confession* are, in essence, the *developed* teaching of Calvin together with the incorporation of Federal Theology.

If we compare the arrangement of the *Institutes* with the *Confession*, we notice that whereas the former begin with the knowledge of God which men may have, the latter moves straight into a definition of Holy Scripture. Probably this reflects the fact that Protestants had emphasised for nearly a century the necessary centrality of the Biblical revelation against the traditions of the Roman Catholic Church.

Also we notice that Calvin explained the doctrine of predestination only when he discussed the appropriation of salvation; the Westminster divines stated the doctrine of predestination before expounding the doctrine of creation and totally apart from the chapters on the doctrines relating to the reception of salvation. This changed emphasis may be traced back to the influence of Beza, who, as we have already noticed, was influenced by the scholastic presentation of predestination.

The influence of the Bezan development of Calvinism in the *Confession* may also be seen in the exposition of the doctrines of original sin, limited atonement and justification. Original sin is explained as including the imputation of the guilt of Adam's first sin and the passing on of a depraved nature (Chapter VI). It is specifically asserted that Christ purchased salvation only for "those whom the Father hath given unto Him" (Chapter VIII), and justification is understood as the imputation of the active and passive righteousness to the elect believer (Chapter XI).

Perhaps the most significant difference between the teaching of Calvin and the Westminster divines is that the latter expound Federal Theology. The *Confession* explains the covenant of works in these words:

> The first covenant made with man was a covenant of works, wherein life was promised to Adam, and in him to his posterity, upon condition of perfect and personal obedience.

As we noted above, this concept came into Reformed teaching from the scholastic doctrine of *lex naturae*.

The Westminster divines did use the idea of the covenant of grace in the same way as did Calvin, making it refer to the historical manifestation of salvation in the Old and New Testaments:

> Man by his fall having made himself incapable of life by that covenant (of works), the Lord was pleased to make a second, commonly called the covenant of grace; whereby He freely offereth unto sinners life and salvation by Jesus Christ, requiring of them faith in Him, that they may be saved.

Nevertheless, the Westminster divines understood this as resting upon the eternal covenant of grace made between the Father and Son. This is seen in the Answer to Question 20 of the Westminster Shorter Catechism:

> God having, out of His mere good pleasure, from all eternity elected some to everlasting life, did enter into a covenant of grace, to deliver them out of the estate of sin and misery, and to bring them into an estate of salvation by a Redeemer.

After the ejection of Puritan ministers from the Church of England in 1662, this combination of High Calvinism and

Federal Theology did remain popular amongst many Nonconformists, especially Independents and Particular Baptists; but, as we noted above, a growing number of Nonconformists, especially Presbyterians, began to adopt a moderated Calvinism, similar to that taught at Saumur, but modified by the "political method" of Richard Baxter.

DOCTRINAL ANTINOMIANISM

The most serious perversion of Puritan orthodoxy was doctrinal antinomianism, which was popular amongst some Puritans between 1640 and 1660, and which was condemned by the Westminster Assembly. It also regained some popularity amongst Nonconformists after 1690. Doctrinal antinomianism is to be distinguished from practical antinomianism, which abuses God's grace and was seen amongst the Anabaptists in Munster in 1534. The system of doctrines that is called doctrinal antinomianism is so described only because the system does possess the possible tendency to cause people who hold it to neglect the practical duties of religion.[34]

Four of the most popular teachers of doctrinal antinomianism were John Saltmarsh, John Eaton, Tobias Crisp and Robert Lancaster.[35] They explained the free grace of God to the elect in such a way as to neglect the Biblical teaching that a Christian has certain responsibilities to God such as daily humbling for sin, daily prayer, continual trust in God and continual love to men. One of their favourite doctrines was eternal justification, by which they meant that God not only elected the Church to salvation but actually justified the elect before they were born. As a development of this they taught that justification in time was merely the realisation that eternal justification was theirs already. Another favourite emphasis was the teaching that the only sure way for a Christian to know he was elect was the voice of the Spirit within his soul saying, "You are elect".

With this brief description of doctrinal antinomianism we close our rapid survey of the major developments of Calvinism from the time of Calvin to the passing of the Toleration Act in

1689. It will be our task in subsequent chapters to show how High Calvinism underwent even more changes until in one particular expression of "Calvinism" any resemblance to authentic Calvinism is difficult to see.

[1] Cf. F. Wendel, *Calvin*, p. 263.
[2] Cf. J. Dillenberger, *Protestant Thought and Natural Science*, pp. 50 ff.
[3] Beza, *Tractationes Theologiae*, Vol. I, pp. 170 ff. for place of decree, and Vol. I, pp. 344, 362, 418 for supralapsarianism.
[4] Calvin, *Concerning the Eternal Predestination* (trans. J. K. S. Reid), p. 125.
[5] Calvin, *Institutes* (trans. H. Beveridge), Book II, Chapter 1, section 6.
[6] Cf. W. Cunningham, *The Reformers and the Theology of the Reformation*, pp. 377 ff.
[7] Beza, *op. cit.*, Vol. I, p. 171.
[8] Breward, "The Life and Theology of William Perkins" (Ph.D. thesis), p. 212.
[9] Cunningham, *op. cit.*, pp. 402 ff.
[10] Cf. A. Ritschl, *A Critical History of the . . . Doctrine of Justification*, p. 251.
[11] Beza, *op. cit.*, Vol. III, pp. 248 ff.
[12] Breward, *op. cit.*, p. 196.
[13] *Ibid*, pp. 37-8.
[14] Cf. J. Murray, *Calvin on Scripture and Divine Sovereignty*, for the opposite opinion; for a detailed study see J. B. Rogers, *Scripture in the Westminster Confession*.
[15] *Works of William Perkins* (1612), Vol. I, pp. 437-8.
[16] Calvin, *Institutes*, III, 14, 19. Cf. Wendel, *op. cit.*, p. 276.
[17] In *Studies in John Calvin* (ed. G. E. Duffield), p. 25.
[18] Bangs, "Arminius and the Reformation", *C.H.* XXX (1961), pp. 155 ff.
[19] *Writings of Arminius* (trans. J. Nichols), Vol. I, pp. 193 ff.
[20] Cf. H. C. Porter, *Reformation and Reaction in Tudor Cambridge*, pp. 277 ff.
[21] Cf. A. W. Harrison, *The Beginnings of Arminianism*.
[22] Calvin, *Commentaries on . . . Jeremiah and Lamentations* (tr. J. Owen), Vol. IV, p. 127.
[23] Cf. J. G. Møller, "The beginnings of Puritan Covenant Theology", *J.E.H.* XIV (1963), pp. 46 ff.
[24] Cf. W. Musculus, *Commonplaces* (trans. J. Man), (1562), p. 120 b.; Z. Ursinus, *The Summe of Christian Religion* (trans. H. Parrie), (1587), pp. 253 ff.; C. Olevianus, *An Exposition of the Symbole of the Apostles* (trans. J. Field), (1581), pp. 52 ff.; *Works of William Perkins*, Vol. I, pp. 164 ff.
[25] Cf. G. D. Henderson, "The Idea of Covenant in Scotland", *E.Q.* XXVII (1955).
[26] There is no adequate survey in English of the rise of federal theology. Apart from the studies already referred to, the following may be found of use.

(*a*) Breward, *op. cit.*, pp. 59 ff.

(b) D. J. Bruggink, "The Theology of Thomas Boston", unpublished Ph.D. thesis, Edinburgh, 1956, pp. 81 ff.
(c) E. H. Emerson, "Calvin and Covenant Theology", *C.H.* XXV (1956).
(d) H. Heppe, *Reformed Dogmatics*, pp. 281 ff.
(e) P. Miller, *The New England Mind, The Seventeenth Century*, pp. 365 ff.
(f) P. Miller, *Errand into the Wilderness*, pp. 48 ff.
(g) G. Schrenk, *Gottesreich und Bund im Alteren Protestantismus Vornehmlich bei Johannes Coccejus*.
(h) L. J. Trinterud, "The Origins of Puritanism", *C.H.* XX (1951).
(i) J. von Rohr, "Covenant and Assurance in Early English Puritanism", *C.H.* XXXIV (1965).

The survey by Schrenk is the most comprehensive but it does not include the English scene.

[27] Rex, *Essays on Pierre Bayle and Religious Controversy*, p. 88. The best study of the doctrines taught at Saumur in this period is F. Laplanche, *Orthodoxie et Prédication. L'oeuvre d'Amyraut*.

[28] In Baxter, *Certain Disputations of right to the Sacraments* (1657).

[29] Cf. J. I. Packer, "The Redemption and Restoration of Man in the thought of Richard Baxter" (D.Phil. thesis), and Chapter III below for an exposition of Baxterianism.

[30] Cf. W. J. Ong, *Ramus, Method and the Decay of Dialogue*.

[31] Cf. K. L. Sprunger, "Ames, Ramus and the Method of Puritan Theology", *Havard Theological Review*, LIX (1966), No. 2.

[32] Miller, *New England Mind, The Seventeenth Century*, pp. 161-2.

[33] The same general teaching on God, Sin and Grace is found in the *Savoy Declaration* (1658), and in the *Particular Baptist Confession* (1689).

[34] In *A Succinct and Seasonable Discourse on the occasions of mental errors* (1691), John Flavell gave a list of ten antinomian errors. They were: 1. Justification is an immanent and eternal act of God. 2. Justification by faith is but a manifestation of what God has already done. 3. It is wrong for Christians to examine themselves to see whether they are in the faith. 4. As all sin has been pardoned, confession of sin is not necessary. 5. God never sees sin in believers. 6. At no time does God ever punish the elect. 7. On the Cross Christ became as sinful as we are, and now the elect are as righteous as He is. 8. Christians should not worry about sin in their lives for these can do them no harm. 9. The New Covenant has no conditions, not even faith. 10. Christians are not to rely on signs and marks of grace in their lives as helps to an assurance of salvation.

There is a similar criticism of antinomianism in Samuel Rutherford, *A Survey of the ... Antichrist* (1648).

[35] Saltmarsh once acted as the chaplain to Oliver Cromwell. Cf. L. F. Solt, "John Saltmarsh. New Model Army Chaplain", *J.E.H.* II. (1951). Eaton was Vicar of Wickham Market, Suffolk. He died in 1641. Crisp was Vicar of Brinkworth in Wiltshire and he died in 1642. Lancaster was Rector of Quarly in Hampshire for a period.

There is a useful discussion of doctrinal antinomianism in Packer, *op. cit.*, pp. 283 ff. Cf. also G. Huehns, *Antinomianism in English History*.

CHAPTER II

THE AUGUSTAN AGE

(TRENDS OF NONCONFORMIST THEOLOGY)

Synopsis: 1. The Seventeenth-Century Background. 2. Deism. 3. Socinianism. 4. Arianism: (a) William Whiston and Samuel Clarke; (b) At Exeter; (c) At Salters' Hall; (d) After Salters' Hall. 5. Rationalism amongst Calvinists: (a) Moderated Calvinism; (b) High Calvinism; (c) Modifications in the Doctrine of the Trinity.

To appreciate the character and development of the High Calvinism taught between 1689 and 1765, we must seek to study and to understand it in the context of the wider, contemporary, theological scene. Therefore in this chapter we shall look at the trends of Nonconformist theology and, where they coincide, at Anglican theology also.[1]

Often the eighteenth century is described as an Augustan age. Nowhere is this more apparent than in the attitudes to religious truth adopted by the theologians of this period. The resulting religious liberalism was not merely a logical outcome of the Toleration Act in 1689, or the freedom of the press after 1695, although both these factors played a part. Its roots went back at least into the middle of the seventeenth century, and probably even into the late sixteenth century when Cambridge theologians debated the doctrines of predestination and free will.[2] These roots grew in the fertile soil of reaction against the "enthusiasm" and "fanaticism" of the Puritan era, and through the influence of Platonism, Latitudinarianism, the new scientific outlook and the philosophy of John Locke.

THE SEVENTEENTH-CENTURY BACKGROUND

"Enthusiasm" was the word commonly used to describe the doctrinaire fanaticism of unbalanced minds. "It arises," wrote John Locke, "from the conceits of a warmed and overweening brain" and "it takes away both reason and revelation, and substitutes . . . the ungrounded fancies of a man's own brain, and assumes them for a foundation both of opinion and conduct".[3] In similar vein, David Hartley (1705-1757) wrote that it "may be defined as a mistaken persuasion in any person that he is a peculiar favourite with God; and that he receives supernatural marks thereof".[4] Thus defined it has particular reference to the sects of the Puritan era but also included the Quakers, with their appeal to the inner light, and the Roman Catholics, with their appeal to the infallible chair.

From a group of Cambridge theologians throughout the second half of the seventeenth century came an important reaction against both the enthusiasm of the Puritan sects and against orthodox Calvinism itself. Since this group had a particular interest in Platonism, its members have been called the Cambridge Platonists. Members of the group included Henry More, Benjamin Whichcote, Henry Cudworth and John Smith.[5] As they believed that true religion is reasonable, they held that the best thoughts of the greatest philosophers of the past could help to illuminate its truth. So it was that they turned to the Greek philosophers, especially to Plato and his followers, believing that their writings constituted a necessary handmaid to the understanding of religion. This appeal to the Platonic concept of reason, with its doctrine of innate ideas, was their most conspicuous characteristic. It involved for them the unification of the whole personality in the pursuit of truth. Their exaltation of reason transcended mere rationalism since their appeal was also to "the inner experience of the whole man acting in harmony not to mere logic chopping which (might) leave conduct and even conviction unaffected".[6] Because they held that truth was one, though mediated through two channels, reason and revelation, there was no conflict in their minds over the relationship of faith and reason. They did not found any particular school of thought but they did make a real contribution to the growth of the idea that toleration of a man's views is an inherent right due to every man.

The word "Latitudinarians"[7] was first used as a designation for the Cambridge Platonists. It is now usually used to describe those Anglicans who were educated by Smith,

Cudworth or More at Cambridge, and who sought to eliminate enthusiasm, dogmatism, irrationality and excessive emphasis on the authority of tradition from religion, and to replace them with a calm, reasonable interpretation of the Bible. Thus men like John Tillotson (1630-94) and Edward Stillingfleet (1635-99) stood for an attitude and a temper rather than for any particular creed. Though they did not abandon the objective side of religion, their emphasis was primarily on a proper moral outlook of life. They tried to meet what they believed were the greatest intellectual and ethical needs of their generation, and, in so doing, they contributed to the changing character of theology from being dogmatic to being rationalistic.

The discoveries of Isaac Newton (1642-1727)[8] showed his generation that the universe was an ordered cosmos governed by one uniform mathematical order. His theories produced in the minds of many people the conviction that there must be a God because of the order and design of His creation. Yet, since Newton's discoveries had broken up the old cosmological theories, which appear in such beautiful dress in Milton's *Paradise Lost*, the temptation to intellectual arrogance by his followers was strong. One serious result of Newton's influence was that God seemed to lose His personal nature as He became the Great Mechanic of a great machine, the world, and the Great Architect of a great building, the cosmos. Later these tendencies helped to foster the growth of Deism and Unitarianism.

If Isaac Newton was the originator of scientific physics, John Locke (1632-1704)[9] was the creator of a scientific philosophy. Beyond the influence of any other man, John Locke was the moving spirit of the eighteenth century. His famous *Essay Concerning Human Understanding* gained great popularity because it said those things which seemed most revelant to the issues and needs felt by those who lived in the Augustan age. Repudiating the old belief that the human mind contains innate ideas, he focused attention on the problem of knowledge and how the human mind receives that knowledge.[10] Skilfully he analysed the powers of the human mind, drawing attention to the things we can truly know rather than those we cannot know. He insisted that the material which the mind uses is provided by the five senses and that thought, itself, is a process conducted in a spirit of detachment, uninfluenced by irrational enthusiasm. If a man begins with self-evident facts, and self-evident propositions, there is no reason why he should not reach results in the religious sphere as reliable as those in the scientific sphere. Thus Locke believed that he could provide the evidence for the existence of God which was equal to mathematical certainty. Unfortunately this idea of God, like the God deduced from Newton's premises, was just the necessary postulate of a series of arguments and deductions. He lacked the glory and lofty splendour of the God of the Puritans. The joint effect of the influence of Newton and Locke was to gain a respectful place for natural religion in English theology, as well as to encourage the enquiry into the nature and authority of divine revelation. Also, as is apparent in his *Reasonableness of Christianity*, Locke wanted to reduce religion to its simplest form. This, he thought, was to believe in God and His Messiah with the amendment of life as a necessary consequence.

Thus it was that many religious men became willing to submit religion wholly to reason because there was everywhere a sublime confidence that reason and revealed religion were in harmony. The old idea, that revealed truths were suprarational without being contrary to reason, tended to fall into the background. From the press, after the licensing system had expired sometime between 1693 and 1695, there came a host of books which sought to present a reasonable or rationalistic approach to Christianity. Men, who in earlier decades would have been persecuted for publishing heterodox views, were now free, within certain limits, to air their opinions. The rational expression and defence of religion became the keynote of the age, and remained so until Joseph Butler (1692-1752) and George Berkeley (1685-1753) insisted that religious truth cannot be proved, and John Wesley (1703-1791) and William Law (1686-1761) implied that reason is irrelevant to true faith, and, finally, David Hume (1711-1776) announced that Christianity cannot rest on reason.[11]

THE AUGUSTAN AGE

As the expression of religious truth in the latter part of the seventeenth century showed a marked reaction against the scholasticism of the Puritan Federal Theology, so many thinkers in the eighteenth century not only continued this trend, but also began to doubt the metaphysical presuppositions inherent in the Nicene and Athanasian Creeds.[12] Also, as the majority of religious men found the Augustinian doctrines of sinful man and irresistible grace distasteful, they adopted the Pelagian and Arminian view that man contributes to his salvation by making an act of his own will to accept the grace of God.[13] In the discussion of the doctrine of God, many old beliefs, condemned by the Church in previous centuries, again appeared and proved popular, as men tried to recover what they considered to be the simplicity of early Christianity. These beliefs included Socinianism and Arianism. To make matters worse, all this took place amongst Christians when Deism was proving attractive to those who were overwhelmed with what they believed was clearly revealed in the world of nature.

DEISM[14]

Deism became widely known in England only after the publication of the English edition of *Christianity Not Mysterious* in 1702, written by John Toland (1670-1722). His ideas, and variations of them, were taken up and exploited, by a few men who caused a stir amongst religious people quite out of all proportion to their numbers or ability. Anthony Collins (1676-1729), Matthew Tindal (1657-1733), Thomas Morgan (*d*. 1743) and Henry Dodwell (*d*. 1784) were men who, having been impressed by Newton's discoveries, saw the universe as governed by immutable laws made by Newton's "Master Physicist", and were unable to reconcile the idea of this Absolute Being with the God of the Hebrews who, according to the Bible, revealed Himself to men like Moses and Elijah. What Roland N. Stromberg has written is true: "What distinguished the deist was not an interest in natural religion, but the belief that natural religion *alone* was sufficient, without need for any Christian revelation".[15] The deist believed that, had Christianity not been corrupted by priests and metaphysicians, it would have agreed with the religion that they deduced from the world of nature. They looked upon Jesus of Nazareth as a good man and an excellent moralist but not as a supernatural, divine being. Though deism flourished in England from 1702 until the middle of the century, it caused the greatest stir amongst Churchmen and Dissenters in the late 1720s and the early 1730s. To answer its claims and to vindicate the need for some form of divine revelation, men of many shades of theological opinion from Socinian to High Calvinist entered into controversy with the deists. But the very fact that the attacks of a handful of men upon traditional Christian beliefs and presuppositions could cause such concern in religious circles, reveals just how low was the spiritual temperature of the nation.

SOCINIANISM[16]

The first challenge to orthodoxy from within the churches, and from those who claimed to derive their teaching from Scripture, came from a few men who had either read the works of Fausto Sozzini (*d.* 1604), or those written by one or another of his followers. After 1688, and until 1703, a continual stream of Socinian tracts flowed from a printing press. The publication of these was probably financed by the philanthropist, Thomas Firmin (1632-1697). Though Anglicans sought to give an answer to them, Dissenters were so embroiled in their own Crispian and Antinomian controversies that they did not, in general, join in the controversy. The word "Socinian" was often used in the seventeenth century to describe anyone who denied the doctrine that Christ made a Satisfaction to God for sin because Socinus himself had made a radical criticism of the usual orthodox doctrine of the atonement. Socinus had also rejected the belief that Christ existed as a divine being before His human birth and, accordingly, he had denied the doctrine of the Trinity. He believed that Jesus Christ was only a creature upon whom God bestowed some form of divine office. Thus the main theme of the Socinian

THE AUGUSTAN AGE 37

tracts in the "Socinian" or "Unitarian" controversy of the 1690s was the doctrine that God is One, not three in One, and that Christ was a creature, though a unique creature.

ARIANISM

William Whiston and Samuel Clarke. Arianism "began a long and uninterrupted course in England through the work and influence of two Cambridge scholars, differing greatly in calibre and temperament".[17] These men were William Whiston, the mathematician, and Samuel Clarke, the metaphysician. Whiston, who had succeeded Sir Isaac Newton as Lucasian Professor, lost his chair in 1710 because of his beliefs which he was not ashamed to make public. In 1711, he published *Primitive Christianity Revived* in four volumes. This work on the early Church and its doctrines helped to prepare the way for "the most memorable work in the history of the Arian movement",[18] Samuel Clarke's *Scripture-Doctrine of the Trinity* (1712). In this book Clarke, the respectable rector of St. James, Westminster, examined the Biblical passages relative to his subject. His conclusion was that, though the Bible does reveal a God in Trinity, supreme worship and honour should only be given to the Father. Though Clarke was correct in his claim that his doctrine was not Arianism (*i.e.* as taught by Arius in the fourth century), those who read his book realised that, at least, he had abandoned the doctrine of the Trinity as stated in the Athanasian Creed. The publication of the *Scripture-Doctrine of the Trinity* caused no small stir in the Church of England; it also proved to be the main source from which Arianism amongst Dissenters grew.

At Exeter. In the city of Exeter there were three Nonconformist congregations, which supported four ministers, and which were controlled by a committee of thirteen laymen. One of the four ministers was James Peirce (1674-1726) who had studied in Holland. Later, when in Cambridge, he had known William Whiston and after this, when a minister at Newbury, had read Clarke's book. Another of the Exeter ministers, Joseph Hallet (1656-1722) kept an academy where several of the students were in correspondence with Whiston and Clarke. One student, Hubert Stogden (1692-1728), who had accepted the new theology, was ordained at Shepton Mallet in Somerset, on the strength of a certificate given to him by James Peirce and other ministers in the area. This incident proved to be the beginning of a controversy in Exeter and also of a series of appeals and visits to London. Peirce refused to give his assent to an article on the Trinity drawn up by local ministers and finally declared that the Son is subordinate to the Father. He also omitted from the public worship of his congregation the doxology which was sung at the end of the metrical psalms. On March 10th, 1719, Peirce and Joseph Hallet, were excluded by the committee of laymen from their pastoral positions.

At Salters' Hall.[19] As communications continued between the Devon and London ministers, the latter, moved by signs of Arianism amongst a few London ministers,[20] began (though not at first deliberately) to arrange themselves into two groups. One group felt that subscription to the orthodox doctrine of the Trinity was necessary in order to preserve purity of doctrine. The other group, though not wishing to deny the doctrine of the Trinity, desired that the words of the Bible be made the standard of Faith, not human interpretations of it, for such they held were the historic Creeds and Confessions of Faith. On the 24th February, 1719, the ministers associated with the General Body of the Three Denominations met to discuss a letter received from Exeter. After some quiet discussion this meeting at Salters' Hall ended in a division. Fifty-three men voted for a resolution which advised that if a minister departed from orthodoxy in regard to the Trinity, the congregation were justified in ending their association with him, whilst fifty-seven voted against sending this advice. The meeting adjourned for a week and at the next meeting those who believed in compulsory subscription by a minister to orthodox Trinitarian doctrine left the meeting, when the moderator refused to allow further discussion of the question. Those who remained drafted a suitable reply to Exeter in which they expressed the view that they could not condemn anyone who stated the doctrine of the Trinity in Scriptural terms. This was rather vague and was meant to be so. It made room for Samuel Clarke's *Scripture-Doctrine of the Trinity*, the second edition of which appeared in 1719. Yet the majority of those who had signed the letter to Exeter had done so because they believed it was in the interests of religious liberty and the right of private judgement. It was not their intention to encourage heresy.

After Salters' Hall. The definite growth of Arianism (by which we mean any system that made the Son subordinate to the Father) was certainly accelerated by the events in Devon and at Salters' Hall. Not a few Presbyterian and Arminian Baptist (General Baptist) ministers were attracted to Clarke's view and in the 1720s many Presbyterian young men joined the Church of England where they believed there was liberty of opinion. Often the Arianism followed after the adoption of Arminian views of sinful man and God's grace. The greatest contributory factor to the growth of Arian and liberal doctrines were the Academies, especially those at Bridgwater, Exeter, Taunton, Kendal, Whitehaven and Findern in the first part of the eighteenth century.[21]

The Arian movement in England reached its climax in the middle of the century at the time when the Arminian doctrines were very popular. Therefore, whilst denying the orthodox doctrine of the Trinity, the leading Arians also often argued against the Calvinist doctrines of predestination and atonement. Such a theological combination is to be found in the writings of George Benson (1699-1762), John Taylor (1694-1761), Nathaniel Lardner (1684-1768), James Foster (1697-1753) and Samuel Bourn (1714-1796). Benson showed his distaste of Calvinism by reviving the story of the burning of Servetus in Geneva in the time of Calvin.[22] Taylor attacked both the Calvinist doctrine of original sin and the doctrine of Christ's Satisfaction to divine justice.[23] Lardner wrote in 1730, but did not publish until 1760, his *Letter on the Logos*, which advocated Arian principles. Foster, one of London's most eloquent preachers, combined natural philosophy with

Arianism in his sermons published as *Discourses on all Principal Branches of Natural and Revealed Religion* (1749). And Bourn's distinct subordination of the Son may be seen in the second volume of sermons he published in 1760.

As the century progressed liberal Christian belief meant for many Presbyterians and General Baptists the transition from Arianism towards Socinianism and Unitarianism.[24] In the first part of the century the philosophy of John Locke was the guiding spirit of the Arians, but gradually some students sent to Glasgow University by the Presbyterians were influenced by the natural philosophy of Francis Hutcheson, who was professor of Moral Philosophy from 1730 until 1745.[25] These students and others introduced views which approximated to the Socinianism of the 1690s but are better described as Unitarianism since they make God, Who is One, to be the First Cause of all that is. Two men in whose writings the change from Arianism to Socinianism is reflected are Moses Lowman (1680-1752) and Samuel Chandler (1693-1766), but the complete transition from Calvinism through Arminianism and Arianism to Unitarianism may be best seen in the experience and the writings of Joseph Priestley (1733-1804). Accompanying the change in theology, Presbyterian Meeting-Houses became Unitarian chapels.

RATIONALISM AMONGST CALVINISTS

We must now retrace our footsteps to the beginning of the century to look at the theological trends amongst those Nonconformists who did not accept the Arminian and Arian tenets. These were the "Calvinistic" Presbyterians, Independents and Baptists. Many Presbyterian and Independent ministers who had been influenced by the appeal of the "Middle-Way" Calvinism of Saumur and of Richard Baxter adopted a moderated Calvinism. This proved popular with those who were of a conservative frame of mind but who sought to keep in touch with the philosophical developments of their age. Edmund Calamy (1671-1732), Daniel Williams (1643?-1716), Isaac Watts (1674-1748) and Philip Doddridge (1702-1751) are examples of men who held this theology. Other ministers, mostly Independents and Baptists, sought to maintain the orthodox High Calvinism of the Puritan era. Amongst this latter group, a minority, influenced by the pressures of the day, took High Calvinism through a logical step to produce what we may call "Hyper-Calvinism", and which we shall study in subsequent chapters.

Yet in all forms of Calvinism there were to be found those who were perplexed by the orthodox doctrine of the Trinity and who sought to modify it in one direction or another. Just what form some of these modifications took we shall discuss below after brief reference has been made to Moderated and High Calvinism.

Moderated Calvinism. Since we shall discuss the theology of Daniel Williams in the next chapter, it will be appropriate here to look at the theology of Philip Doddridge, who was only a boy when Williams died. Roger Thomas has written that Philip Doddridge "was not an original thinker . . . he owed some of the most liberal elements in his own ways of thinking to his teachers, men who were makers of a liberal tradition, which he inherited from them and maintained with full conviction of its worth".[26] The two men whom Mr. Thomas sees as having influenced Doddridge were Samuel Clark, minister of the Dissenting congregation in St. Albans to which Doddridge was admitted in 1719, and John Jennings, tutor at the Dissenting Academy at Kibworth, which he attended. These men introduced him to the philosophy of John Locke and this helped him to lay a rational foundation for his faith. They taught him to adopt a liberal attitude towards the explication of "mysteries" of the Christian faith and to avoid dogmatism. Also they introduced him to Moderated Calvinism, a combination of Calvinism and Arminianism, which had little to say about predestination and limited atonement or irresistible grace. Rather it emphasised the experience of Christ and could sing:

> O happy day, that fix'd my choice
> On thee, my Saviour, and my God!
> Well may this glowing heart rejoice
> And tell its raptures all abroad.

When Doddridge became a theological tutor he tried to pass on to his students this personal joy in religion as well as the conviction that Christianity is reasonable and is not best expressed dogmatically.

High Calvinism. The rationalistic tendencies towards Arminianism and Arianism did not go unnoticed by the more orthodox Calvinists. Indeed, the popularity of these heterodox views shocked them! A group of influential laymen decided to sponsor a series of lectures in defence of what they considered to be the main doctrines of the Protestant faith. The well-known philanthropist, William Coward (*d.* 1738), seems to have provided the finance and nine ministers, seven Congregationalists and two Baptists, were chosen to give the lectures in the Lime Street Meeting-House each week from 12th November, 1730, until 8th April, 1731. In the preface to the printed version of the lectures[27] the following words appeared:

> When doctrines of pure revelation are opposed, it is the duty of all who believe them, to appear in their defense; and this is really engaging in a noble cause: It is standing up for the honour of the great God, against those who set their imperfect reason and proud conceits, above infinite wisdom: To strive for the faith once deliver'd to the saints, is most necessary, when it meets with the contradiction of sinners. As error never raged with greater violence than it does in our unhappy times, and as lukewarmness never discover'd itself more than in the present day of darkness, it never could be more expedient than now to plead for the glorious gospel of the blessed God. The sufficiency of the light of nature is warmly contended for by such as do not profess to reject revelation; and most of the doctrines of Scripture have been given up, one after another, by some who yet declare that the Bible is their religion. It is therefore now time, if ever, for those who see no reason to renounce the old Protestant doctrines, to bear their testimony against the errors of the day, and to stand up for the great truths, which have been handed down to them by their fathers, and which they embrace, not merely because they have received them from the worthies who have gone before them, but because, after strict and impartial examination, they find, that these, and no other, are the doctrines reveal'd in Scripture.

Since several of the lecturers had previously dealt with the subjects of the Trinity and the Person of Christ in books and sermons, eight of the ministers dealt with the Reformed doctrines of eternal election, particular redemption, Christ's suffering, justification by grace, efficacious grace in conversion, the final perseverance of the saints and the resurrection of the dead.[28] Apart from giving the lectures of the doctrine of justification, Robert Bragge, the minister of the Church which met in the Lime Street Meeting-House, delivered the introductory lecture to the whole series. Abraham Taylor, who became the tutor at the Academy controlled by the newly-formed King's Head Society, gave lectures on three subjects; the insufficiency of natural religion to gain salvation, that true religion does not lead to immorality, and the reasons for the decay of practical religion in the early part of the eighteenth century.

Modifications in the doctrine of the Trinity. Not a few "Calvinists" found the doctrine of the Trinity as explained in the traditional Creeds and Confessions difficult to accept. In his lectures on the *Larger Catechism*,[29] Thomas Ridgley, minister of the Congregational Church which met at the Three Cranes, Thames Street, London, revealed that he found two orthodox positions untenable. He believed that the expressions "the eternal generation of the Son" and "the procession of the Holy Ghost" were absurd and unscriptural phrases. He thought of the Second Person of the Trinity as Son of God by virtue of His office as Mediator and not through eternal generation by the Father. Yet he did not deny the equality of the Son with the Father and His proper eternity.

In his *The Glory of Christ Unveil'd* (1706), Joseph Hussey set out his belief that the human nature of Jesus Christ existed in heaven from the agreement of the covenant of grace by the Trinity. He believed that the verses in Proverbs 8. 22 ff. referred to the Second Person as God-Man possessing the human nature before the creation of the world.[30]

Isaac Watts, who had maintained a neutral position in the subscription controversy at Salters' Hall, found himself confused by the doctrine of the Trinity for most of his life. It was in 1725 that he first gave a clear statement of his view that a human soul was joined to the Second Person of the Trinity in heaven before the creation of the world. He believed that the human race, in its creation, was modelled by God on this archetype, the God-Man, the Mediator, Who became "the first born of all creation" (Col. 1. 15). Then from Mary, the God-Man received His human flesh and form. This Christology also appeared in his *The Glory of Christ as God-Man* (1746).

In the strange book, *The Redeemer's Glory Unveil'd* (1733), by Samuel Stockell, who was once a member of Hussey's Church, we find a combination of Hyper-Calvinism and the doctrine of the pre-existence of the human soul of Christ. Since several writers, apart from Watts, advocated the doctrine of the pre-existence of Christ's human soul it is possible that Stockell was influenced by one or other of these.[31] He believed that it was only correct to speak of the human soul of the God-Man as begotten of the Father. "I cannot understand," he wrote, "the terms in vogue amongst us namely, *eternal Generation* and *essential Filiation*. Because I am positive that Christ, as the eternal God, was never *begotten*, since it is impossible for me to conceive the *Begetter* and the *Begotten* to be of equal date."[32]

Thus we see that the first half of the eighteenth century was a period in which rationalism and latitudinarianism were consciously, or, in some cases, unwittingly, absorbed by men of every theological and philosophical opinion. Though a minority did cling to the Reformed doctrines of predestination and irresistible grace in conversion, the majority of Christians, Nonconformists and Anglicans, favoured the Arminian scheme of universal redemption and man's co-operation with divine grace in conversion. And whilst a few Christians did resolutely hold to the Nicene and Athanasian definitions of the Trinity, a greater number felt it was wrong to impose any form of compulsory subscription to them.

---

[1] For the historical background see D. Coomer, *English Dissent under the Early Hanoverians*.
[2] Cf. Porter, *op. cit.*, p. 282.
[3] Locke, *Essay concerning human understanding*, Book IV, Chapter 19, Section 3.

[4] Hartley, *Observations on Man* (4th ed. 1801), Vol. I, pp. 290-1.
[5] For a study of this group see F. J. Powicke, *The Cambridge Platonists*.
[6] W. R. Inge, *The Platonic Tradition in English Religious Life*, p. 52.
[7] Cf. G. R. Cragg, *From Puritanism to the Age of Reason*, p. 61.
[8] Cf. L. T. More, *Isaac Newton*, for details of his life.
[9] Cf. N. Kemp Smith, *John Locke* for details of his life and thought.
[10] Cf. J. W. Yolton, *John Locke and the way of ideas*, who makes the point that Locke, in repudiating innate ideas, was not so much departing from Descartes as from the prevailing philosophy of English writers, the Cambridge Platonists, for example.
[11] Cf. Cragg, *Reason and Authority*, pp. 93 ff. and 155 ff.
[12] In such words as "substance", "begotten", and "uncreated". The Athanasian Creed (Quicunque Vult) begins with the assertion that he who does not accept its teaching "without doubt shall perish everlastingly".
[13] It was the Dutch version of Arminianism which was popular amongst Dissenters in the eighteenth century and this had its origins at the University of Amsterdam.
[14] For full details of Deism, cf. L. Stephens, *History of English Thought in the Eighteenth Century*, Vol. I.
[15] R. N. Stromberg, *Religious Liberalism in Eighteenth Century England*, p. 55.
[16] For the history of Socinian thought in England throughout the seventeenth century see H. J. McLachlan, *Socinianism in Seventeenth Century England*.
[17] Colligan, *Arian Movement in England*, p. 31.
[18] *Ibid*, p. 34.
[19] Cf. R. Thomas, "The Non-Subscription Controversy amongst Dissenters in 1719: the Salters' Hall debate", *J.E.H.* IV (1953), pp. 162 ff.
[20] Martin Tomkins was relieved of his duties as pastor at Stoke Newington in 1718 for alleged Arianism.
[21] Cf. O. M. Griffiths, *Religion and Learning*, p. 129. For the academies, see H. McLachlan, *English Education under the Test Acts*, and Ashley Smith, *The Birth of Modern Education, 1660-1800*.
[22] Cf. Colligan, *op. cit.*, p. 96. John Brine defended the attitude of Calvin in his *Vindication of some truths of Natural and Revealed Religion*, Chapter 5.
[23] *E.g.* in Taylor, *Scripture-Doctrine of Original Sin* . . . (1738).
[24] Cf. Griffiths, *op. cit.*, pp. 136 ff.
[25] *Ibid*, p. 71.
[26] Thomas in *Philip Doddridge* (ed. G. F. Nuttall), p. 122.
[27] *A Defense of some important doctrines of the Gospel* (1732).
[28] The eight were: Robert Bragge, John Sladen, John Hurrion, Peter Goodwin, Thomas Bradbury, Thomas Hall (Congregationalists) and Samuel Wilson and John Gill (Baptists).
[29] They were published under the title, *Body of Divinity* in 2 vols., 1731-1733.
[30] For more detail see Chapter IV.
[31] *E.g.* Robert Fleming, *Christology* (1708), Vol. III; Henry More, *Magni Mysterii Pietatis* in *Opera Theologica* (1675); Edward Fowler, *Discourse of the descent of the Man-Christ from heaven* (1706).

[32] Stockell, *Redeemer's Glory* . . ., p. 41. Stockell was the minister of the Independent Church, which met in Red Cross Street, from about 1730 to 1753. For a study of the Hyper-Calvinist Christology see P. Toon, "The Growth of a Supralapsarian Christology", *E.Q.* XXXIX (Jan., 1967).

PART TWO

HIGH CALVINISM BECOMES
HYPER-CALVINISM

CHAPTER III

ANTINOMIANISM AND HIGH CALVINISM
(1689-1706)

Synopsis: 1. Controversy 1690 to 1700: (a) The Crispian Controversy; (b) The Merchants' Lecture and "Happy Union"; (c) The case of Richard Davis; (d) The Antinomian Controversy. 2. The Law of God. 3. The Satisfaction of Christ. 4. Federal Theology. 5. Justification. 6. Assurance. 7. The Preaching of the Gospel. 8. The Effects of the Controversy.

The last decade of the seventeenth century witnessed two heated theological controversies in England. Within the Church of England the publication of Socinian tracts caused great alarm and much thought about the doctrines of the Trinity and the Person of Christ. Amongst London Dissenters two apparently similar, yet basically different, doctrines of grace, the one advocated mainly by Presbyterians, the other mostly by Independents, came into serious conflict. Though these controversies were conducted entirely separately, the effects of the Socinian denial of Christ's atoning work were felt in the controversy of the Dissenters. After a brief account of the historical development of the controversy amongst the Dissenters, we shall examine the doctrines around which the heat of disagreement was centred.

CONTROVERSY 1690 TO 1700

The Crispian Controversy. Dr. Tobias Crisp had died in 1642 but his sermons were still popular in 1689 amongst certain Independents. Mr. Marshall, an undertaker, wrote to Samuel Crisp, a son of Tobias Crisp, suggesting that he should assist in the republication of his father's sermons. Samuel Crisp agreed and in the winter of 1689-90 there came from the printing press *Christ alone exalted, being the compleat works of Tobias Crisp, D.D.* There were fifty-two sermons, eight of which had never been previously published.[1] To convince the public that the eight additional sermons were authentic, a certificate was placed in the volume signed by twelve London ministers.[2] This stated that these sermons had "been faithfully transcribed from (Crisp's) own notes". Richard Baxter, who had long opposed all forms of, and tendencies towards, doctrinal antinomianism, deeply resented both the action of Samuel Crisp in editing the book and the twelve ministers for seemingly commending it. In his lecture at Pinners' Hall on 28th January, 1690, he condemned the Crispian doctrine of the imputation of sin to Christ as an error, and also accused the ministers of "hanging up a sign to show where Jezebel dwelt".[3] John Howe, one of the twelve signatories, was quick to defend himself in a pamphlet entitled *Some considerations of a certificate* (1690). Baxter wrote a reply to this but did not publish it since seven[4] of the twelve ministers published an explanatory letter in John Flavell's book, *A Succinct and Seasonable Discourse* (1691); part of this book contained an attack on doctrinal antinomianism. The ministers explained that they had signed *only* to vouch for the integrity of Samuel Crisp as a copyist. In an effort to show that his father's doctrine of imputation was Biblical and orthodox, Samuel Crisp wrote *Christ made sin* (1691), which he addressed to the merchants who financed the lectures at Pinners' Hall.

Richard Baxter died in 1691. His successor as unofficial leader of those who taught a moderated Calvinism was a Welshman, Daniel Williams,[5] who had recently arrived in London from a pastorate in Dublin, and who was the pastor of the Presbyterian congregation that met in Hand Alley. From early 1691 he had plans to write a book to expose the errors that he believed were to be found in the sermons of Tobias Crisp.

The Merchants' Lecture and the "Happy Union". At the Glass House in Old Broad Street (renamed Pinners' Hall when the Pinners' Company, makers of pins and needles, bought it), a weekly lecture supported by merchants had been held since 1673. There were six lecturers, four Presbyterians and two Independents.[6] In the years previous to the Toleration Act of 1689, one of the reasons for the lecture was to demonstrate the essential unity amongst Dissenters. This unity came to have more positive form, first in 1690 with the foundation of the Common Fund to help needy country churches, and secondly in 1691 when most of the London Presbyterian and Independent ministers decided to form the "Happy Union", to call themselves the "United Ministers", to hold regular assemblies and to assent to certain articles of Faith and Order.[7] Yet, within four years the Merchants' Lecture, the Common Fund and the "Happy Union" had ceased to exist in their original form. In their lectures at Pinners' Hall, first Thomas Cole,[8] pastor of the Congregational Church meeting in Silver Street, and then Nathaniel Mather, pastor of the Congregational Church meeting in Paved Alley, defended similar doctrines to those which Baxter had condemned, and in reply Daniel Williams attacked the views of Cole and Mather. At a special meeting of subscribers at Pinners' Hall in August, 1694, it was decided to expel Williams from the lectureship.[9] Out of sympathy for Williams, and to demonstrate Presbyterian solidarity, the three other Presbyterian lecturers left with Williams in order to form a new lecture at Salters' Hall, which was planned to take place at the same time as the original lecture. Because of differences over the doctrines of justification by grace, and also because of differences concerning the power of synods (brought into sharp relief by the case of Richard Davis), the Congregational ministers decided in late 1692 to discontinue to meet with the Presbyterians. They also withdrew from the Common Fund and started a Fund of their own. Several efforts were made in the next four years to reunite the two parties but they were without success.[10] The fact was that each party was becoming progressively entrenched in its own theological dogmatism, on the one hand in a moderated, "Middle-Way",[11] Calvinism, and, on the other hand, in High Calvinism, partially modified by doctrinal antinomianism.

The Case of Richard Davis. Having been born in Wales, Richard Davis was a schoolmaster in London until 1689. In early 1690 he became pastor of the Independent Church at Rothwell, near Kettering in Northamptonshire.[12] Like his former pastor, Thomas Cole, he was a strict Congregationalist in regard to Church polity and a rigid High Calvinist in his doctrinal views. Furthermore, he possessed that evangelical fervour which has helped to make many Welsh preachers famous. He made Rothwell into a centre for aggressive evangelism. Riding on horseback, as John Wesley was also soon to do, Davis and his lay helpers preached in many towns and villages in the surrounding counties. Many complaints were sent to the United Ministers of London about both what he preached and how he evangelised. To vindicate himself he went twice to London and on the second occasion, May, 1692, he met the full assembly of the United Ministers. He was accused by Daniel Williams of various errors but no definite decisions were taken concerning him. Later in that same month Daniel Williams published his book, *Gospel-Truth Stated and Vindicated wherein some of Dr. Crisp's opinions are considered*, which he hoped would check the propagation of the teaching of Davis as well as Crisp. Soon after, a deputation which included Williams, went from London to Kettering to enquire into the complaints against Davis. Both Davis and his Church refused to attend this enquiry which they dubbed "The Ketterin-Inquisition". He was accused of various doctrinal errors as well as dividing churches and sending out ignorant, illiterate preachers.[13] Yet neither this enquiry, nor at least three pamphlets written against him, were sufficient to stop his preaching for he had friends in London and converts in the country who looked to him as their spiritual guide.[14]

The Antinomian Controversy. Before the preface to the first edition of *Gospel-Truth Stated*, there appeared a certificate signed by sixteen Presbyterian ministers claiming that Williams had "rightly stated the Truths and Errors".[15] Though many Congregational ministers, with some Particular Baptists, were not in total agreement with everything Crisp had said, they did feel that it was safer to err on the side of exalting of God's free grace than to err (as they believed) with Williams in teaching salvation partly by works.[16] They were quick to provide replies to Williams's book. Thus began eight years of replies and counter-replies. William Lorimer, Vincent Alsop, John Humfrey and Samuel Clark, with the two Anglicans, John Edwards of Cambridge, and Edward Stillingfleet, Bishop of Worcester, supported Williams.[17] The chief opponent of Williams was Isaac Chauncy, who had been educated at Harvard College, and was minister of the Congregational Church in Mark Lane. Thomas Cole, Robert Traill, Thomas Goodwin, Jnr., Stephen Lobb, all Congregational ministers, and two Baptists, Benjamin Keach and Thomas Edwards, stood firmly behind Chauncy.[18] Several men including John Howe, Thomas Beverley, Samuel Young, and two Dutchmen, Herman Witsius and Jacobus Keyser, did their best to mediate and reconcile the parties.[19] The main points of controversy were the doctrines of justification and Christ's Satisfaction, and developing out of these doctrines such questions as: Is the covenant of grace conditional? Is the Gospel a new law of grace? And when does justification take place?

The doctrine of Christ's Satisfaction for sin came into prominence after 1695 because Stephen Lobb accused Richard Baxter and Daniel Williams of favouring the Socinian denial of the orthodox doctrine of the suffering of Christ. To those not versed in the ramifications of Reformed theology the whole controversy seemed unintelligible.[20] After the deaths of Thomas Cole and Nathaniel Mather in 1697, some of the heat was taken out of the debates. They finally came to an end (apart from a few murmurings from the country) in 1700, after a group of leading Congregational ministers had publicly declared against antinomianism and Daniel Williams had written *An End to Discord* (1699). Yet the "Happy Union" was never restored.

The doctrines to which we shall pay particular attention in the following exposition are those which describe God's law, Christ's Satisfaction for sin, God's covenants, justification, assurance and the preaching of the Gospel. Since the publication of Crisp's sermons was a contributory cause of the controversy, our method will be first to outline Crisp's teaching, secondly, by way of contrast, to give the views of the "Middle-Way" Calvinists, and finally to discuss the doctrines of those who defended Crispian doctrines because they believed that they were identical with, or at least very similar to, High Calvinism.

THE LAW OF GOD

The basic, underlying difference of opinion in the Antinomian controversy concerned the nature of the law of God. Since his purpose was to extol Christ and free grace, Crisp had little to say about the moral law. The following quotation shows that he believed that God's justice is affronted by human transgression of His law, although he never seems to have explicitly stated that God's law is an eternal expression of His righteousness and justice.

> When Adam sinned, and by that act involved himself, and his whole posterity, into a state of transgression; nay, into a constant course of enmity and rebellion against God; by which justice was extremely violated and Divine majesty insufferably affronted; it concerned God for the maintenance of the honor of justice, to take order for the reparation of the violation and affront of it.[21]

He believed that the law served a useful purpose in convincing men of their need of a Saviour; nevertheless, he gave it little or no place in the life of a Christian since he held that "free grace is the teacher of good works".[22]

Richard Baxter and those who shared his views (*e.g.* Daniel Williams and William Lorimer) proceeded on the assumption that God's moral government of the world is the central subject of theology. God is a Rector and a Governor: His law is a means to an end, and, therefore, He may change it as He will, providing His true end is attained. Dr. J. I. Packer describes Baxter's view in the following way:

> When man had fallen and God purposed to glorify Himself by restoring him, He carried out His plan not by satisfying the Law, but by changing it. God's Law is thus external to Himself. The penal law of works with its sanction of death for sin was enacted not because it was a natural and necessary expression of the divine character, but simply because efficient government required it. The demand for retribution was grounded in the nature of government, rather than in the nature of God and could be dispensed with if it seemed wise.[23]

On the basis that God's law is changeable, Baxter taught that the law of nature ("the law of innocency"), which was in force before the fall of man, was different from the law of grace which came into force after the fall.

Like his fellow Independents and Particular Baptists, Isaac Chauncy held the orthodox Calvinist doctrine of God's law. For a definition of this we may turn once more to Dr. Packer.

> To orthodox Calvinism, the law of God is the permanent, unchanging expression of God's eternal and unchangeable holiness and justice. It requires perfect obedience from mankind on pain of physical and spiritual death, and confers salvation and eternal life only upon those who perfectly obey it. God could not change this law or set it aside in His dealings with men without denying Himself. When man sins, therefore, it is not God's nature to save him at the law's expense. Instead He saves sinners by satisfying the law on their behalf that He might continue just when He becomes their justifier.[24]

In his catechism, *The Doctrine . . . according to Godliness*, Chauncy gave the essence of the above doctrine in the answers to three questions.

> LXVII. *How doth God dispense justice?*
> (a) In Legislation or in making Laws or Covenants and in execution of those Laws; in doing of both He doth right to Himself and the Creature.
> LXVIII. *How doth God do justice to Himself in Legislation?*
> (a) In taking to Himself that sovereign power over the Creature which by natural right belongs to Him.
> LXIX. *How doth God dispense justice to the Creature?*
> (a) In dealing with it according to His Law in a faithful distribution of rewards, or punishments, as they become due.[25]

The two doctrines of grace which came into conflict in this controversy only become meaningful to modern ears when they are considered as resting upon the two conceptions of God's law, the Baxterian and the orthodox Calvinist. It was because these two views were irreconcilable that the two parties only were able to agree to differ after a decade of heated debate.

THE SATISFACTION OF CHRIST

Fourteen of Crisp's sermons were based on the words of Isaiah 53. 6, "The Lord hath laid upon him the iniquity of us all". Crisp's critics believed that he taught that Christ on the Cross was an *actual* sinner as He bore the sins of the elect in His own body. Whilst his language does at times seem capable of such an interpretation, he did not really mean to say this. As he himself put it:

> The meaning is that Christ himself becomes the transgressor in the room and stead of the person that had transgressed; so that in respect of the reality of being a transgressor, Christ is really the transgressor, as the man that did commit it was, before he took it upon him. Beloved, mistake me not; I say, not that Christ ever was, or ever could be, the actor or committer of transgressions, for he never committed any; but the Lord laid iniquity upon him; and this act of God's laying it upon him, makes him as really a transgressor, as if he himself had actually committed it.[26]

In order to stress the fact that, in Christ, God has blotted out the sins of the elect, Crisp tended to speak rather too literally about the imputation of sins to Christ (and also of Christ's righteousness to the elect).

To appreciate the doctrine of Christ's Satisfaction for sin held by the "Middle-Way" Calvinists, we must refer once more to the views of Richard Baxter since these were held, at least in outline, by men like Daniel Williams. Baxter taught that Christ, as Priest, offered His death to God, as Rector, as the ground for the relaxation of the original penal law of the covenant of works. He believed that Christ did render a certain satisfaction to divine justice, but this was only a nominal equivalent of the penalty due to man; that is, it was something which God was pleased to accept as such. (This allowed Baxter to introduce the Gospel as a new law; we shall discuss this later.) "God's laying our sins on Christ," wrote Williams, "is a moral Act of God as a Rector, *i.e.* he agreed and appointed that Christ should in His person stand obliged to bear the punishment of ours that we might obtain pardon."[27] Yet he denied that God reckoned the elect to be united to Christ in His sinless, righteous life and atoning death: "I deny that Christ by His obedience made atonement as a proper Pecuniary Surety in the Law of Works".[28] Rather, Williams believed that Christ obtained atonement for sin by obeying the mediatorial law which He undertook to fulfil in His agreement to the covenant of redemption. Also the "Middle-Way" Calvinists believed that by His humiliation and death Christ achieved universal redemption.

The orthodox, Reformed doctrines of election and law entered into the High Calvinist explanation of Christ's Satisfaction for sin. First, it was held that Christ made satisfaction for the elect only. He died to satisfy divine justice only for those whom the Father had given to Him. Secondly, it was stressed that Christ died to make satisfaction to God, the Just and Righteous One, for the breach of the holy law of God. Just as it is technically possible in a court of law for one man to pay the debts of another who is found guilty, so the High Calvinists held that Christ paid the debts of the elect by acting as their Surety. By His righteous life He satisfied the precepts and commands of the moral law, and in His death He suffered the curse and punishment due to the elect as transgressors of the law. Thus it was believed that Christ as the Surety of the elect not only fulfilled the obligation within the covenant of works to keep the moral law perfectly, but He also suffered the curse which that covenant passes on all who fail to meet its requirement.

Chauncy looked upon the resurrection of Christ as the proof that God had discharged Christ from the guilt of sin imputed to him and (since Christ was the Surety of the elect) had discharged the elect as well.

> It was the will and purpose of God and Christ that upon Christ's satisfaction for sin, he (Christ) should have an immediate discharge, and all the elect virtually and really in him a general discharge, but not (yet) manifested and personally applied to particular persons.[29]

This "general discharge" of the elect was sometimes referred to as "virtual justification" and we shall have cause to refer to it again below. Though Chauncy defended Crisp's doctrine of imputation of sins to Christ, he carefully explained that Christ was not considered by the Father as an actual sinner. The guilt of sins was imputed to Christ but the sins were not transfused into Him.

XXXVI. *Doth not Transacting Sin thus on Christ make him a sinner by Transfusion?*
a. The Transaction of anothers sin, speaks the contrary. He is still said to bear our sins and not his own, which Transaction is common in all Acts of Suretyship, where the Surety is not looked upon by the Law or any other, as the Contractor of the Debt, but only one that becomes a Debter for and instead of the Principal.[30]

Furthermore, Chauncy denied that Crisp taught that Christ removed the pollution of sin, as well as the guilt of sin, from the elect. Rather the pollution of sin is gradually removed through the sanctifying work of the Holy Spirit.

Federal Theology

Tobias Crisp accepted the general outline of Federal Theology that God entered into a covenant with Adam, including all his descendants in him, and a covenant with Christ, including all the elect in Him. However, as he desired to exalt grace and depreciate the idea of salvation by works, he saw the Mosaic Covenant and the New Covenant as essentially different, and not diverse administrations of the one covenant of grace as the majority of divines believed: "They are two distinct covenants of grace; they are not one and the same covenant diversely administered, but they are two distinct covenants".[31] This brief quotation reveals the basic weakness of all doctrinal antinomians. They failed to appreciate what Dr. E. F. Kevan has recently called "the Grace of Law".[32] In regard to the New Covenant Crisp emphasised that, as far as the elect were concerned, it had absolutely no terms or conditions.

The "Middle-Way" Calvinists held the general principles of Federal Theology as taught by the Saumur school, and more specifically by Richard Baxter. They believed that the covenant of works was only in force whilst Adam was innocent, but after the fall, God, as Rector, brought in the law of grace. Salvation for the world was planned in eternity by God in Trinity in the form of a covenant of redemption. In this contract God the Son agreed to become man and to die for the sins of the world. God the Father agreed to accept His humiliation and death as a sufficient payment for the sins of the

ANTINOMIANISM AND HIGH CALVINISM

whole world. They believed that the covenant of grace was proclaimed in the preaching of the Gospel. This covenant was the proclamation that Christ had died and gained forgiveness for all those who repent of sin and believe on His name. They called the Gospel-covenant the "law of grace" or the "new law" (hence the name "neonomians") and held that the Gospel itself commanded sinners to repent and to believe in Christ. To strengthen their case they pointed out that in some Old Testament passages the Gospel is called a "law": for example, Isaiah 42. 4. "The isles shall wait for his law."[33]

Isaac Chauncy went into great detail to define the meaning of the word "covenant" both in legal and Biblical usage.[34] Like the other High Calvinists he preferred to speak only of two essential covenants, the covenant of works and the covenant of grace. He held that the requirements of the moral law within the covenant of works remained in force after Adam's fall and were binding on all Adam's descendants. This belief naturally followed from the conception of the law of God as an eternal expression of His righteousness.

The High Calvinists taught that the terms and conditions of the covenant of grace were settled in eternity. The Father chose the elect out of the (future) race of men; the Son covenanted to become man and, as the Surety of the elect, to satisfy the requirements of the covenant of works on their behalf; the Spirit agreed to regenerate those for whom Christ died and to convey to them the gift of faith so that they could believe on Christ. Thus they argued that, as far as the elect were concerned, the covenant of grace had no conditions. The only conditions within it applied to Christ as Mediator. By His fulfilling of the conditions, He gained for the elect, and for the the elect only, the forgiveness of sins and acceptance with God the Father, as well as the sanctifying graces of the Holy Spirit.

Conscious that the *Larger Catechism* had used the word "condition",[35] Chauncy felt obliged to explain his own position. He believed that the Westminster divines did not make "faith a condition of the covenant of grace, but only of interest, reception or participation of the said covenant". They meant no more than *modus recipiendi* or *participandi* or that faith is only an instrument, was his conviction.[36] In the controversy the High Calvinists constantly affirmed that faith is not a "foederal condition". Chauncy wrote at times as though he believed that the covenant of grace in its constitution was nothing but the eternal decree of election in larger form, and that the same covenant in its execution in time was only the working out of the decree in the world. This logical, though unscriptural position, had been previously held by such men as Johannes Maccovius in the Arminian controversy, and William Ames had used the distinction of the covenants of redemption and grace to avoid such an error.

JUSTIFICATION

The Crispian doctrine of justification may be seen as taking place in three stages. First, in the eternal covenant of grace, the elect, as they existed in God's mind, were justified on the basis of the certainty of the work of Christ. Secondly, the elect were justified in Christ, their Head, in His triumphant resurrection from the dead. Finally, justification by faith through which the individual conscience of the elect person is assured that in God's sight he has always been justified. Tobias Crisp believed that this way of understanding the doctrine glorified the free grace of God and made it impossible for man to contribute to his salvation. At times he spoke as though the elect became as righteous as Christ Himself and this upset his opponents.[37]

In his sermons published as *Man made Righteous by Christ's obedience* (1694), Williams gave a definition of justification.

> What is it to be made righteous by Christ's obedience?
> 1. To be made free from condemnation, as if we had not sinned and to be entitled to acceptance with God and eternal glory, as if we had kept the whole Law. . . .
> 2. By the merits and Spirit of Christ to be made obedient to the Gospel, at least in those things which Christ hath graciously appointed to be

the conditions of our enjoyment of saving benefits, as the effects of Christ's sole righteousness.[38]

The "Middle-Way" Calvinists believed that the ground of justification was in the life and death of Christ. By obeying the conditions of the new law of grace the believer is enabled to receive the effect of Christ's righteousness. They explained the words of Paul in Romans 4. 22, "Therefore (his faith) was imputed to him for righteousness", as meaning that since Abraham obeyed the Gospel condition of faith, he was made righteous in regard to the law of grace.

Despite the similarity between the Crispian and High Calvinist doctrines of justification, the latter was more carefully explained. The High Calvinists looked upon justification as a forensic act of God. To the elect believer God reckoned the active obedience of Christ as the ground of his acceptance before divine justice, and the passive obedience of Christ as the ground of His forgiveness. Nathaniel Mather expressed it like this:

> This Suretiship Righteousness of Christ which is through Faith upon believers, is his perfect conformity to the Moral Law in all that which the Justice of God did by virtue thereof demand on behalf of the Elect from Christ as their Surety; that they might not only in a way of Grace, but in a way of Justice be brought to that Eternal Blessedness and Glory whereto God in his infinite love had appointed them.[39]

Whilst Mather and Benjamin Keach only discussed justification by faith in their printed sermons on the subject, Chauncy defended the doctrines of eternal and virtual justification.

XXXVI. *When is it that a Sinner is justifyed?*
a. God eternally decreed a sinner's Justification, and Christ was an Eternal Surety (by Vertue of the Covenant of Grace) for Sin; through which Suretyship the Saints before his coming in the flesh were justifyed; and lastly, Christ and all the Elect in him were justified at His resurrection, or else he could not have arose from the dead.[40]

Chauncy also believed that justification by faith was basically only an inward persuasion that justification was already achieved and settled in heaven.[41] But sometimes he expressed himself more carefully:

XXXIX. *What place hath Faith in Justification?*
a. It is no other than a Spiritual Organ in a quickened Sinner, freely given to him, and wrought by the Holy Spirit in and through Jesus Christ, whereby he Sees, Tastes, and Feelingly lays hold on Jesus Christ, and his Righteousness for Justification.[42]

Apart from Chauncy, both Thomas Cole and Richard Davis seem to have been favourably disposed to the doctrine of eternal justification.[43]

Assurance

With regard to the means by which the elect soul may have an assurance of eternal salvation, Crisp had no hesitation in affirming "that it is the Spirit of Christ, and the faith of the believer only, that immediately call the soul, and testify to it its interest in Christ, and so give sufficient evidence to it". Concerning the usefulness of good works as testimonies to election, he believed that they might "come in as handmaids to bear witness to the thing" but he added that they were inferior testimonies.[44]

Daniel Williams expressed the view of the "Middle-Way" Calvinists in the following way:

> The ordinary way whereby a man attaineth a well-grounded assurance, is not by immediate objective revelation; or an inward voice saying, Thy sins are forgiven thee: But when the believer is examining his heart and life by the Word, the Holy Spirit enlightens the mind there to discern faith and love, and such other qualifications which the Gospel declareth to be infallible signs of regeneration . . .; and according to the evidence of those graces, assurance is ordinarily strong or weak.[45]

This view is just the reverse of Crisp's doctrine.

Isaac Chauncy's position was somewhere between the Crispian and "Middle-Way" Calvinist views:

> I affirm that the witness of God in His Word, and the Spirit in the heart firmly believed, is, and produceth, the greatest assurance for firmness and durability in the world. . . . And as for other grounds of comfort and assurance which arise from the visibility of the grace of God, and the fruits of the Spirit in the heart and life, I highly value them, as subordinate grounds for comfort and assurance.[46]

He believed that a Christian would never have assurance if he looked only at his good works.

THE PREACHING OF THE GOSPEL

Crisp's method of preaching seems to have been to offer Christ freely to men and to invite them to find in Him their forgiveness and eternal life. He had little sympathy for those preachers who waited for signs of repentance before offering grace. He offered grace immediately.

> I know I may speak that which will be offence to some, but I must speak the truth of the Lord, whatever men say. I say, whatever thou art in this congregation, suppose a drunkard, a whore-master, a swearer, a blasphemer, and persecutor, a madman in iniquity, couldst thou but come to Jesus Christ; I say, come, only come, it is no matter though there be no alteration in the world in thee, in that instant when thou dost come; I say, at that instant, though thou be thus vile as can be imagined, come to Christ; he is untrue if he put thee out; "In no wise (saith he) will I cast thee out".[47]

The weakness of Crisp's method in the view of his critics was that he failed to give sufficient place to the law of God in convincing men of their need of a Saviour.

The "Middle-Way" Calvinists believed in the free offer of the grace of Christ to sinners but with certain qualifications. Daniel Williams explained that these were "a renouncing of sin and idols and denying carnal self", and they also included "a conviction of sin and misery and some humblings of soul". Concerning the purpose of offers of grace he held that "the declared design is that they (the hearers) may be willing to accept of Christ and so partake of an interest in him".[48] As we noted earlier, they believed that the Gospel itself, as a law of grace, commanded men to repent and believe.

Isaac Chauncy held a view very similar to that of Crisp. As the ways of the Spirit of God are not known to men he wrote that "we are not to prescribe any methods or measures of humblings, much less to say such and such moral virtues or duties are necessary requisites or qualifications before a sinner comes to Christ". The purpose of the offer of Christ to men is that when the elect "are come to Christ they should know that faith was not of themselves . . . but from Christ".⁴⁹ Thomas Goodwin, Jnr., carefully pointed out that the command of the Gospel to men, calling them to repentance, came from the moral law, which was first given to Adam and then codified in the law of Moses. The High Calvinists believed that the Gospel itself was the good news of free grace but that it made use of the moral law in its commands to sinners.⁵⁰

Yet it does seem that amongst some uneducated London lay preachers the notion was being put forward that preachers were not to invite all their hearers to receive the grace of Christ since that grace was only intended for the elect. The five Congregational ministers,⁵¹ who signed the *Declaration . . . against Antinomian Errours and Scandalous Persons intruding themselves into the Ministry* (1699), regarded it as a serious error. In 1692 Richard Davis had been accused of the same error but had denied that he only offered Christ to the elect.

Having studied some of the major doctrines of grace taught by the High Calvinists involved in the controversy, we are in a position to ask an important question. It is: Were the doctrines defended and advocated by the High Calvinists in the controversy the same as those set out in the statements of faith prepared by the Westminster Assembly of divines? The simple answer is that they were not all the same. At least in the books of Chauncy, Cole and Davis there are emphases and views which were not approved by the Westminster Assembly of divines. These relate to the doctrines of justification and assurance, and as we have already noticed, to the emphasis on the unconditional nature of the covenant of grace.

To ascertain the teaching concerning justification we may quote from the *Westminster Confession of Faith:*

> God did, from all eternity, decree to justify all the elect; and Christ did, in the fulness of time, die for their sins, and rise again for their justification. Nevertheless, they are not justified until the Holy Spirit doth in due time actually apply Christ unto them.⁵²

This statement rules out the doctrine of eternal justification as taught by such men as William Twisse, William Pemble and

ANTINOMIANISM AND HIGH CALVINISM

the doctrinal antinomians.[53] It also means that Chauncy, and to a lesser extent Cole and Davis, were teaching a doctrine that the greater number of orthodox Puritans regarded as erroneous.[54] The fact that the doctrine of eternal justification was gaining popularity amongst some Christians at the end of the seventeenth century may be seen in the Congregational *Declaration* against the following as an error:

> That the Eternal Decree gives such an existence to the Justification of the Elect, as makes their Estate, whilst in unbelief to be the same as when they do believe, in all respects, save only as to the Manifestation; and that there is no other Justification by Faith, but what is in their consciences.

Whilst the Westminster Standards do not deny the doctrine of virtual justification for the elect in the resurrection of Christ, they do not explicitly teach it, although it is to be found in the writings of such Puritans as William Ames and Thomas Goodwin.[55]

The Westminster divines held that assurance of salvation was attainable by the Christian through three channels.[56] These are, in order of importance, first a firm trust in the certainty of the divine promises of salvation; secondly, the evidence of such virtues as faith, hope and love in the life; and thirdly, the witness of the Spirit with the human spirit that a particular person is a child of God. In his defence of Crispian doctrines Chauncy gave a different order of priority to the means by which a person may have assurance. He gave equal priority to faith in God's promises and the inner witness of the Holy Spirit and made the evidence of virtues a subordinate ground for assurance. Though this change may seem to be a minor one, it does witness to the fact that more emphasis was being laid on God's grace and the work of His Spirit, with less emphasis on the duty of a Christian to do good works as his responsibility to God.

THE EFFECTS OF THE CONTROVERSY

Apart from the disruption of the "Happy Union", the Common Fund and the Merchants' Lecture, the controversy served to harden each side in its respective theological position.

On the one side, "Middle-Way" Calvinism was looking more like Arminianism, and on the other, High Calvinism seemed to be absorbing doctrinal antinomianism. In 1692 Robert Traill had pithily written that "such men that are for middle ways in points of doctrine have a greater kindness for that extreme they go half-way to, than for that they go half-way from".[57] This proved true of both parties. "Middle-Way" Calvinism went half-way in some cases towards Arminianism and later became Arminianism and sometimes Arianism. High Calvinism went half-way towards Crispianism and in some cases turned into Hyper-Calvinism.

In concluding we may suggest three way in which the doctrines of the modified High Calvinism, labelled as "antinomianism" by Daniel Williams, spread in England. First, the sermons of Crisp and the books written by his defenders were read in many parts of Britain as well as on the continent of Europe and in New England. As Chauncy wrote more than any other man his influence was probably the greatest. Secondly, several of the ministers (*e.g.* Chauncy and Goodwin)[58] taught in Academies where they had influence over young men intended for the ministry. Finally, there was the preaching of Richard Davis and his lay preachers. Daniel Williams admitted that their influence spread to thirteen counties. Therefore the seeds were sown which, when watered after 1706 by the doctrines of Joseph Hussey, grew, in some cases, into an even more rigid form of Calvinism, Hyper-Calvinism.

[1] Earlier volumes of his sermons were published in 1643 (fourteen sermons), 1644 (seventeen sermons), 1646 (eleven sermons) and 1683 (two sermons). The fifty-two sermons were reprinted in 1755 (edited by John Gill), 1791 and 1832.
[2] They were: Vincent Alsop, Richard Bures, John Gammon, John Howe, Thomas Powell, John Turner (Presbyterians); Isaac Chauncy, George Cokayn, George Griffith, Increase Mather, Nathaniel Mather (Independents); and Hanserd Knollys (Baptist).
[3] Cf. S. Crisp, *Christ made sin*, pp. 1-2.
[4] The seven were: Howe, Alsop, N. Mather, I. Mather, Turner, Bures and Powell. Both Knollys and Cokayn died in 1691. The reply of Baxter is still in manuscript and may be read in Dr. Williams's Library. (Baxter MS., 59. 11 ff, 24-6.)
[5] Cf. R. Thomas, *Daniel Williams, "Presbyterian Bishop"*.

ANTINOMIANISM AND HIGH CALVINISM 67

[6] Cf. T. G. Crippen, "The Ancient Merchants' Lecture", *T.C.H.S.* VII (1916). The original six were: Richard Baxter (who preferred the title 'Nonconformist'), Thomas Manton, William Bates, William Jenkyn (Presbyterians), John Owen and John Collins (Independents).

[7] Thomas Cole, Richard Taylor and Nathaniel Mather did not join the Union. For the basis of union see *Heads of Agreement assented to by the United Ministers in and about London* (1691). For details of the Common Fund see A. Gordon, *Freedom after Ejection*.

[8] Samuel Crisp stated that Mr. Cole once said: "If I had but a hundred pounds in all the world, and could not get that book of Dr. Crisp's under fifty pounds, I would give it, rather than not have it; for I have found more satisfaction in it than in all the books in the world besides, except the Bible". Preface to *Christ made sin.*

[9] Cf. R. Thomas, "The Break-up of Nonconformity", in *Beginnings of Nonconformity*, p. 56.

[10] Especially by John Howe. Cf. Thomas, *Daniel Williams . . .*, pp. 19-20.

[11] The term "Middle-Way" was first used by John Humfrey as a description of Moderated Calvinism in the title of several pamphlets.

[12] Cf. N. Glass, *The Early History of the Independent Church at Rothwell.*

[13] For his own account of the proceedings see R. Davis, *Truth and Innocency Vindicated* (1692), pp. 47 ff.

[14] The first attack upon Davis was by P. Rehakosht (John King), *A Plain and Just Account of a most horrid and dismal plague at . . . Rothwell* (1692). After the Congregational ministers had left the "Happy Union" those who remained published *The Sense of the United Ministers concerning Richard Davis* (1692). And G. Firmin wrote *A Brief Review of Mr. Davis's Vindication . . .* (1693).

[15] The second edition had forty-eight signatures in September, 1692.

[16] *E.g.* Benjamin Keach, *Marrow of True Justification* (1692), p.8, stated: "I had rather erre on their side who strive to exalt wholly the free grace of God than on their side who seek to darken it . . .".

[17] See *D.N.B.* for Alsop, Humfrey, Clark, Edwards and Stillingfleet. Lorimer was the Presbyterian pastor at Lee in Kent. In 1695 he was invited to become professor of theology at St. Andrew's University, but due to the plague there he never took up the appointment.

[18] See *D.N.B.* for Chauncy, Cole, Traill, Lobb and Keach. Thomas Goodwin, Jnr., pastor at Pinner, was the son of the famous Puritan of the same name. Thomas Edwards (1649-1700) was a Welshman and a member of the Wrexham Nonconformist Church of which Daniel Williams was once a member. Donald Wing, *Short Title Catalogue 1641-1700*, confuses this Thomas Edwards with Thomas Edwards (1599-1647), father of John Edwards of Cambridge.

[19] See *D.N.B.* for Howe. Beverley was minister of the Independent Church which met at Cutlers' Hall, Cloak Lane. Samuel Young came from South Molton, Devon, to take part in the closing stages of the controversy. Keyser and Witsius were Dutch professors and the latter had been in 1685 the chaplain to the Netherland Embassy in London.

[20] *E.g.* John Locke, *The Reasonableness of Christianity* (ed. I. T. Ramsey), p. 76: "I have talked with some of their teachers, who confess themselves not to understand the difference in debate between them . . .".

[21] Crisp, *Works* (1832), Vol. II, p. 14.

[22] This is the title of Sermon XLV, Vol. I, p. 317.
[23] Packer, *op. cit.*, pp. 303 ff.
[24] *Ibid.*
[25] Chauncy, *Doctrine according to Godliness*, p. 26.
[26] Crisp, *op. cit.*, Vol. I, p. 269. Cf. S. Crisp, *Christ made sin*, for very similar views.
[27] Williams, *Gospel-Truth Stated*, pp. 7 ff.
[28] Williams, *Man made righteous* . . . (1694), p. 92.
[29] Chauncy, *Neonomianism Unmask'd* (1693), Vol. II, p. 47.
[30] Chauncy, *Doctrine according to Godliness*, p. 172.
[31] Crisp, *op. cit.*, Vol. I, p. 251.
[32] He called his study of the Puritan doctrine of law, *The Grace of Law*.
[33] Cf. Lorimer, *An Apology for the ministers* . . . (1694), who gave a learned defence of the Baxterian concept of law and grace.
[34] Chauncy, *Neonomianism Unmask'd*, Vol. II, pp. 108 ff.
[35] The answer to Q. 32 has the phrase "requiring faith as the condition".
[36] Chauncy, *op. cit.*, Vol. II, p. 146.
[37] Crisp, *op. cit.*, Vol. II, pp. 204 ff. Sermon XXXVII, "Christ's righteousness alone dischargeth the sinner".
[38] Williams, *Man made Righteous* . . ., pp. 50 ff.
[39] Mather, *The Righteousness of God through Faith* (1694), pp. 7-8.
[40] Chauncy, *Doctrine according to Godliness*, p. 231.
[41] Chauncy, *Neonomianism Unmask'd*, Vol. II, p. 227.
[42] Chauncy, *Doctrine according to Godliness*, p. 232.
[43] Cf. Cole, *The Incomprehensibleness of Imputed Righteousness* (1692), and also, *A Discourse of Christian Religion* (1692), pp. 342 ff., and Davis, *Truth and Innocency Vindicated*, p. 47. They both held that the elect were justified from eternity "in the purpose of God". It is possible that Chauncy's threefold justification for the elect, in eternity, in Christ's resurrection, and in the conscience, originated in (or, at least, was confirmed by) the rigid application of Ramism to the doctrine of justification. In the "Epistle to the Reader" of his *Doctrine . . . Godliness*, he described his theological method as "Amesian" or "Richersonian". No doubt he learned his Ramist methods (as interpreted by Ames and Richardson) at Harvard College. Threefold justification would seem to fit in well to the threefold classification of ideas in technologia. The archetypal idea of justification in God's decrees is eternal justification; the entypal idea of justification in living entities is virtual justification in Christ, and both these as perceived, the ectypal idea, is conscience-justification. See above Chapter I.
[44] Crisp, *op. cit.*, Vol. II, p. 79. The title of the sermon is "Inherent Qualifications are doubtful evidences for heaven".
[45] Williams, *Gospel-Truth Stated*, p. 160.
[46] Chauncy, *Neonomianism Unmask'd*, Vol. II, pp. 331-2.
[47] Crisp, *op. cit.*, Vol. I, p. 213.
[48] Williams, *op. cit.*, pp. 80 ff.
[49] Chauncy, *op. cit.*, Vol. II, p. 208.
[50] Cf. Goodwin, *Discourse of the True Nature of the Gospel* (1695), pp. 45 ff.
[51] They were: George Griffith, Stephen Lobb, Matthew Mead, John Nesbitt and Richard Taylor.

[52] See Chapter XI, Section iv.
[53] Though Twisse was prolocutor of the Westminster Assembly for a short period his views were not shared by the majority of divines present. Pemble gave up the doctrine of eternal justification before he died. Cf. R. Baxter, *Richard Baxter's Apology* (1654), p. 323.
[54] Cf. Thomas Watson, *A Body of Divinity* (1692), reprinted 1965, p. 228. "Are we justified from eternity? No: for (1) By nature we are under a sentence of condemnation, John iii. 18. We could never have been condemned if we were justified from eternity. (2) The Scripture confines justification to those who believe and repent . . . Acts iii. 19. Therefore their sins were uncancelled and their persons unjustified till they did repent".
[55] *E.g.* Ames, *Marrow of Sacred Divinity* (1642), pp. 114 ff., and Goodwin, *Christ set forth*, in *Works* (1862), Vol. IV, Section iii, Chapter V.
[56] *West. Conf. Faith.* Chapter XVIII.
[57] Traill, *Vindication of the Protestant Doctrine of Justification*, in *Works* (1810), Vol. I, p. 253.
[58] Cf. J. W. Ashley Smith, *Birth of Modern Education*, pp. 92 ff. and p. 295. Chauncy was the tutor of the new Congregational Fund Academy, established in 1701, and Goodwin kept students in his home at Pinner.

CHAPTER IV

NO OFFERS OF GRACE
(THE THEOLOGY OF HUSSEY AND SKEPP)

Synopsis: *Joseph Hussey:* 1. 1660-1694: Years of Preparation. 2. 1694-1705: Years of Reading. 3. 1706-1707: The Birth of Hyper-Calvinism: (*a*) Supralapsarianism; (*b*) God-Man Christology; (*c*) Irresistible Grace; (*d*) Criticism; (*e*) Influence of Hussey's theology.
John Skepp: 4. (*a*) The true nature of conversion; (*b*) The inability of human power to effect conversion; (*c*) The Spirit's energy in conversion; (*d*) Influence of Skepp's theology.

One of the witnesses who appeared at the "Ketterin-Inquisition" in 1692 was Joseph Hussey from Cambridge. He gave evidence to show that Richard Davis had caused a division in the Congregational Church at Cambridge, and that preachers from Rothwell were setting up meetings in towns and villages far removed from Rothwell.[1]

This connection with the action of the United Ministers of London at Kettering must have caused Hussey to follow with interest the subsequent controversy in London, which we described in the last chapter. Certainly in 1706 he expressed the view that Richard Baxter's criticism of Crispian doctrines in 1690 was the "first *Thunder Clap* in *Pinners' Hall*" of the subsequent troubles.[2]

Since Joseph Hussey holds a strategic position in the creation of Hyper-Calvinism in England, we shall devote the first part of this chapter to an examination of his views. To make the account of his theology as interesting as possible, and to see how and why his doctrines developed as they did, we shall trace their development from his conversion experience in 1686 up to the publication of his two influential books in 1706 and 1707.

JOSEPH HUSSEY[3]

1660 to 1694: Years of Preparation. Joseph Hussey was born at Fordingbridge, Hampshire, on 10th April, 1660.

JOSEPH HUSSEY

Here, as a boy, he was educated by Robert Whitaker,[4] a Nonconformist minister who had left the University of Cambridge in 1661. He continued his education at the Newington Green Academy, where the tutor was Charles Morton, who later became the Vice-President of Harvard College, New England.

Looking back on his spiritual experience in these formative years he wrote:

> I had been from a Child Sober, well Educated, constantly read the *Scriptures*. . . . I pray'd *secretly* upon my Knees to God . . . from five or six years old: (Later) I wrote sermons, I pray'd longer. I read Mr. *Allein's* Works, Mr. *Baxter's* Books, &c., and the more I grew in acquaintance with these the more I vehemently suspected I had committed the Unpardonable Sin. . . .
>
> God directed me by his providence to Mr. Charnock's book (*Discourse on the existence and attributes of God*). And what was it I found in that book converted me? Why, the *Spirit* of Christ turning me in a moment to the Lord, in managing this one point, *Everlasting Love* to me in the Covenant which the Father made with the Son before I had a *Being*, I saw; yea, before the foundation of the world.[5]

This conversion experience took place in 1686 some five years after he had preached his first sermon, which, according to his Diary,[6] was preached in London on 14th August, 1681.

Before his ordination by six Presbyterian ministers on 26th October, 1688, which took place (as he carefully recorded in the Diary) when William of Orange was under sail to England, he served as chaplain to a rich lady in Clapham and Sir Jonathan Keate, of the Hoo, Hertfordshire. After a brief pastorate at Hitchin, he moved to Cambridge to become pastor of a Presbyterian congregation there. Concerning 19th November, 1691, he wrote in his Diary: "the day of my setting apart in the Church to the pastoral office . . . Mr. Scandrett, of Haveril preached and other ministers (Mr. Robert Billio, of St. Ives, and Mr. John King, of Wellingborough) prayed".[7]

Soon after his arrival in Cambridge, Hussey persuaded the Church members to adopt Congregational principles of Church government. The entry in his diary for 4th October, 1694, reads:

> At a church meeting in my house, I opened Proverbs 27. v. 23: "Be thou diligent to know the state of thy flocks, and look well to thy herds". After this we openly practised Congregational order.

It would seem that he had reconsidered Church order in the light of his newly-found appreciation of the doctrine of God's everlasting love to the elect. At least, in retrospect, he wrote in 1706 that his experience was:

> I love his *Government*, which before I hated: now I love his *ordinances*, and Christ's Yoke, *Church-Order*, which I find all my *Old Religion* a meer stranger to, being cut out more for the *Gentleman* than the *Believer*.[8]

Perhaps reflection about the controversy surrounding Richard Davis had caused Hussey to make the decision to adopt Congregational Church order in preference to Presbyterian order.

In 1693, at the request of a Presbyterian friend, whom he did not name, Hussey published a course of sermons preached from the fourteenth chapter of the Gospel of Luke. The book was entitled *The Gospel Feast Opened*. He sought to establish three points of doctrine in the book. These were: first, that the Gospel is a large Feast stored with all kinds of spiritual provision; secondly, that God makes an invitation to sinners to come into this Feast; and thirdly, that the Gospel is a Feast whose provisions are now ready. Whilst the doctrinal framework is clearly that which is contained in the *Westminster Confession of Faith*, the sermons place great emphasis on God's invitation to sinners to accept the Gospel of Christ. He described the properties of Christ's invitation to unconverted sinners as a gracious invitation, a free invitation, a sovereign invitation, a clear invitation, a commanding invitation, an open invitation, a large and comprehensive invitation, a pressing, earnest invitation, a seasonable invitation and an effectual invitation to the elect.

1694 to 1705: Years of Reading. In the midst of his preaching and pastoral duties in and around Cambridge, Hussey gave himself to a comprehensive study of the development of theological dogma. From the references in his books, we know that this study included some of the writings of Athanasius, Arius, Augustine, Clement and Nestorius from the early fathers, Aquinas, Bradwardine and Lombard from the medieval scholars, and Amyraldus, Arminius, Beza, Calvin,

Gomarus, Luther, Maccovius and Socinus (with many others) from the continental reformers, as well as most English Puritans and not a few Roman Catholic writers of the sixteenth and seventeenth centuries. Thus in 1706 he felt free to write:

> I declare, therefore, that wherein I go contrary to many Good Men, I do it after an *examining* of their writings, and weighing books at the *Sanctuary Scales* (a labour that hath been now upon my hands more than *Ten* Years past) and good reason, to go by God's *Word* and *Spirit* at last, having been carried away with much *Deceit* in many *other writings*, and by too many of some of our good men who have found more Goodness to mean well, than judgement to open all well they have undertook.[9]

Though Hussey did not explain the reasons which caused him to read so widely from 1694 to 1705, it is not difficult to see what these probably were. The Antinomian controversy in London raised many of the issues which Protestants had debated throughout the Reformation era, and the Unitarian controversy in the Church of England focused attention upon the orthodox definitions of the Christian faith, the Nicene and Athanasian Creeds. Indeed, as we noted in Chapter II, the whole theological and philosophical scene in the Augustan age was one of enquiry, doubt and turmoil. Hussey, it would seem, set himself the task of finding truth, and, at least to his own satisfaction, he thought that he had found it.

1706 to 1707: the Birth of Hyper-Calvinism. In these two years Hussey published two books. The first, nearly one thousand pages in length, was entitled *The Glory of Christ Unveil'd or the Excellency of Christ Vindicated* (1706). In the second, *God's Operations of Grace but No Offers of His Grace* (1707), he developed and elucidated a doctrine briefly mentioned in the first. These books contain those doctrines which Hussey felt embodied the clear and distinctive teaching of the Bible. Before we discuss them below, it will be instructive to notice the attitude he had come to hold concerning much of the theological dogma produced in the Christian era.

> What ignorance is there in our *Systems* of Divinity! What defects in our *Catechisms* and Confessions! What barren heaps in our *Librarys*![10]

Amongst these barren heaps was the book he had published in 1693 for he wrote that it was "the same General *Tradition* of men and books" which had mistaught him fourteen years previously.[11] Yet some glimmers of pure Gospel light had shone, he believed, in the writings of the orthodox side in the "*Latine Controversies* of the Gospel" (*i.e.* the Arminian controversy in Holland in the early seventeenth century).[12] His general distrust of books had come after a spiritual revelation when he felt that Christ had clearly led him "into more of the love of the Father, the knowledge of himself, and the operations of the Spirit". In his mind's eye, he saw a clear vision of salvation planned and achieved by God in Christ before the creation of the universe. He summarised his position in the following way:

> For mending the disorders which old *Adam* and his Posterity cannot by fallen Nature alter, I have, by Grace, chosen the *Supra-Lapsarian* (or *Over-Fall*) way, in the everlasting Love of the Father to the elect in His Son, *Jesus Christ*, whom he loved as the *Mediator* between God and them, *before the foundation* of the world. I have seen both Beauty and Antiquity in the *Wisdom-Mediator:* His *Supra-Lapsarian* Constitution in the Will and Grace of God as *Wisdom-Mediator* was the Foundation of his Consequent *Sub-Lapsarian* Constitution in the same Will and Grace, as *Redemption-Mediator* [on earth]. Accordingly I see my *Supra-Lapsarian* relation to him . . . was the Foundation of my *Sub-Lapsarian* relation to God, to bring my person safely, by his own means, thro' all the Ordered changes of the fall, till all he hath settled *for* me be made perfect in glory *to* me.[13]

We shall only be able to understand this strange theology if, first, we consider three of its distinctive features, the supralapsarianism, the doctrine of the God-Man, and the concept of irresistible grace to the elect.

(*a*) *Supralapsarianism.* Because of the Arminian controversy, the two Reformed presentations of the doctrine of predestination, supralapsarianism and infralapsarianism (sublapsarianism), were more logically defined. Hussey read these "*Latine Controversies*" and decided to adopt the supralapsarian presentation of predestination and thereby followed in the steps of Beza, Perkins and Twisse, as well as various Dutch divines.[14] Thus he believed that the decree of election preceded the decree to create man and permit the fall:

> God would therefore ordain, after and under *his predestinating us to the Adoption of Children by Jesus Christ unto Himself* upon the bottom of *Election-Union* in Christ Jesus, that these Creatures should fall, and out of the Miserable *Fall* rise by Grace the happiest Creatures that ever came into God's thoughts.[15]

Often he referred to the thoughts and settlements of God concerning the salvation of the elect as the "Over-Fall" way and spoke of the redeeming work of God on earth as the "Under-Fall" way. As none of the major Reformed statements of faith contain the doctrine of supralapsarianism, it was probably this omission that he had in mind when he complained: "What defects in our *Catechisms* and Confessions!"

(*b*) *God-Man Christology*. His Christology developed out of his doctrine of predestination. Although the full details of his doctrine of the God-Man would have been suggested to him by the reading of many books, the writings of Thomas Goodwin seem to have influenced him the most. Of these, the *Exposition of Ephesians I*, and the treatise *Of the Knowledge of God the Father and His Son Jesus Christ* are the most important.[16] Referring to Goodwin's admiration for a view of Christ which stressed his real manhood, and the union of the divine with the human nature Hussey wrote:

> Rare it was until Dr. Goodwin's *Folio-Works* came out on the *Ephesians* to meet with any one who would venture to call him the *Man*. . . . I say, till then, I did never believe into the *Man* standing in the Second Person of God, nor could thereby apprehend the human nature was any more than a quality and an arbitrary denomination of Christ which men had got up, and not the very substance of the Mediator.[17]

Perhaps it should be added that the doctrine of the God-Man which Goodwin gave in his *Exposition of Ephesians I* is developed into a rather more logical form in the treatise, and it was probably from the former not the latter that Hussey received inspiration. At least he denied that the latter actually influenced him.[18]

Thomas Goodwin set the Augustinian and Calvinist doctrine of the Mediator, the God-Man, in the context of the Ramist and Puritan doctrine of technologia. As we noted in Chapter I, the foundation of this doctrine was the belief that in the mind of God there existed and exists a coherent and rational scheme of ideas upon which He modelled the world.

Apart from the verses in the first chapter of Ephesians which speak of predestination and Christ, Goodwin found the basis for his doctrine in Colossians 1. 15-19; John 17. 5, 24; and Proverbs 8. 22-9. All these passages make some reference, he believed, to the Second Person as He existed in heaven before the creation of the universe and after the agreement of the covenant of grace. He thought that these verses describe the Second Person as the God-Man (that is possessing the human nature) in the mind of God as an archetype, a real, pre-existent idea. Christ was thus "set up from everlasting"; when God "marked out the foundation of the earth" the God-Man was by Him. He was "the image of the invisible God, the first-born of every creature" as He existed in God's decrees.

> The Son of God was extant and with God at the instant when he was chosen to this glory of being God-Man; ... the glory of it was immediately given to him at the very act of predestinating him to it.[19]

Goodwin also believed that when God created the human race He modelled it on the idea He already had of the God-Man. Indeed, not only was Adam formed in the image of the God-Man (Genesis 1. 26), but his marriage to Eve was a type of the union of Christ to God's elect already ratified in heaven. The elect in heaven had already been given as "meet companions, children, and spouses unto him" since in God's thoughts He was already set up as an "everlasting father and . . . an everlasting husband to them".[20]

It must be emphasised that Goodwin was not saying that Christ's human nature actually existed in heaven. Rather, as he explained:

> Whatever God predestinates, persons, or things concerning persons He hath the idea thereof and all that appertains thereto in the divine mind.[21]

Goodwin was simply trying to explain what thoughts of God were contained in the decrees of predestination.

Joseph Hussey regarded his own vision of the glory of

Christ in the decrees of God as the most important revelation which God had given to him. This is seen in the following words:

> Reason by thinking to give us the best and brightest and most honourable Conceptions of God, hath run into the most unaccountable Absurdities and Inconsistencies with the best reasoning of all; that is, *Divine Revelation*, and all because the Holy Ghost hath not led men, even such Men as have been our Leaders, into this *Marvellous Light* of Christ as the *Glory-Man*, standing in God before *the foundation of the world*.[22]

Like Goodwin, Hussey accepted the orthodox doctrine of the eternal generation of the Son of God, but he went one step further than Goodwin by making a distinction between the words "eternal" and "everlasting".

> As the Son of God in his Personal Relation in God's *Nature* is from the Days of Eternity without beginning: so the Son of God in God's *Covenant* is the *Wisdom of God* from Everlasting in *another* sense, that is, *adoptive* and *consequent*, and hath some beginning with God: even in the *Beginning of His Way, before His Works of old*, as the *Alpha*, and the First Work of them all.[23]

What Hussey was trying to say was that, though the Second Person is an eternal being, the God-Man is not, since He only came into "existence" with the agreement of the covenant of grace.

In days when the doctrine of the Trinity was being abused by some and misunderstood by others, Hussey felt that he had found the key to a perfect appreciation of the doctrine. Rather than seeking to understand a "few hard *School Terms*" (*e.g.* "consubstantial")[24] Hussey felt that:

> The *Trinity* is not to be studied or known but as we mingle the Doctrine of *Christ* with that High or Glorious study, and bring along with us the *Wisdom-Mediator*, as the human nature had a *secret way* to stand in God, and so was the *Glory-Man* from the Days of Everlasting.[25]

Therefore to know the doctrine of the "Glory-Man" was to possess the secret of the mystery of the Trinity.

Concerning the relation of the God-Man and the Church in the decrees of God, Hussey explained:

> As the Eternal Son of God in the Everlasting Covenant and Counsel of Settlements did assume or take on him the *Covenant-Man* (or first Human

Nature from which *our* Natures flow) into union with *Himself*, the *Second Person*; so did he take the Church presented of God unto him in a *Marriage-Deed* of Settlement and *Covenant-Contract*, at the Donation of the Father, and before the *Holy Ghost*: consequently *Christ* and the *Church* were both mystically *One Person* in God's covenant, long before *Adam*. . . . This was the *Secret Glory* of the Church in her *Marriage Settlements* between God and Christ.[26]

Also, believing that the Scriptures were to be understood in their plain, literal sense and not allegorised, he explained that the passages in Isaiah which describe the Suffering Servant of Yahweh referred not to a future person (after Isaiah's time), but to what was already past and settled in God's decrees. He thought that "the sufferings of Christ . . . are laid open . . . as the *History* of what was then past to God, than as a Prophecy of what was . . . to come to men".[27]

It is very difficult to know whether or not Hussey did believe that the human nature of Christ mysteriously existed "standing in God" before the Incarnation. The truth seems to be that Hussey gave a greater supralapsarian emphasis both to the doctrine of the God-Man and to the covenant of grace with the result that the "ideas" and the "archetypes" of technologia became in his thought *real* persons and things. Hussey tried, as it were, to make a synthesis of God's thoughts and decrees in eternity, and from everlasting. Concerning his theological method he said:

> The Order I follow is *Synthetical* to bring what may be joined more aptly and *Unitedly* under the same Head together, after this Model, *Person* and *Things*, rather than *Analytical*, to resolve the more Material Particular as to a Thing, before I have sometimes done with what perhaps is of less moment, as to a *Person*.[28]

From a study of part of the "over-fall" way, we must now turn to a facet of the "under-fall" way.

(c) *Irresistible Grace*. The view that saving grace is irresistible and therefore only available for, and to be offered to, the elect is developed in detail in *God's Operations of Grace but No Offers of His Grace*. Though Hussey could have claimed that some Reformed theologians had taught supralapsarianism, and that his Christology was similar to Goodwin's, he could claim no support from earlier writers for his view that only the elect are to be invited to accept the grace of God. The doctrinal antinomians against whom the five Congregational ministers published their *Declaration* (1699) had not, as far as can be ascertained, written against the free offer of Christ, although they had mentioned it in their preaching. Hussey gave three basic reasons for rejecting the usual Reformed and Puritan view of the free offer of Christ to men in the preaching of the Gospel. In shortened form these were:

1. In the Bible Noah is described as a "preacher of righteousness" and the apostles as ordained preachers. Paul described himself as "appointed a preacher and an apostle" (I Timothy 2. 7). To preach Christ is thus Scriptural, whilst to offer Him is not. "Concerning offers we may say one thing it lacketh, and that is texts of Scripture to prove that proffering and preaching are, in the sense of the Holy Ghost, the same thing".[29]

2. To offer grace and salvation to sinners will not help them to become Christians, since it is the irresistible grace of God alone that makes Christians. "The Spirit's working an ability in sinners is an operation of God's grace; He works under the imputation of the righteousness of Christ to the elect, according as God has chosen them in Him."[30]

3. As the elect were given to the Son by the Father, and the Son to the elect in eternity, the gifts that accompany saving faith, the Holy Spirit and eternal life, are only given to those for whom they are intended. Therefore to offer the gifts of God's grace to everybody in preaching is wrong for they are only intended for the elect.[31]

In view of these arguments we may well ask, "How then is the Gospel to be preached if the grace of Christ is not to be offered to all, and all are not to be invited to receive Christ as their Lord and Saviour?" Hussey anticipated this question and gave a detailed reply. He believed that the doctrines of the Gospel were to be preached to all, but the grace of God was not to be offered to all.

We must lay open the things of God, to the glory of God in Christ, to the glory of God by Christ, to the glory of God through Christ. In Him, in the deeds and settlements of God the Father. By Him, in the purchase and conveyance as God-Man Mediator. And through Him, in the spring of influence even through Christ, by the Spirit, which are quite distinct from speculations concerning Christ.[32]

After this definition he proceeded to give a list of twenty propositions which described his beliefs concerning the contents and the true manner of preaching the Gospel. They were:[33]

1. We must preach the Gospel, as it agrees with the reconciliation of God to sinners and sinners to God, through the gift by grace, in the imputation of the righteousness of God in Christ to them.
2. We must preach the Gospel, as the Gospel is the way or means of God's bestowing the Holy Spirit on the elect, and the only way and means of exalting the gift of God. God's gift of the Spirit must be exalted, but an offer exalts not the gift of God's Spirit, the gift bestowed.
3. We must preach the Gospel as it is most fitted to the display of effectual grace. To offer God's grace is to steal: God saith, Thou shalt not steal.
4. We must preach the Gospel evangelically, so as, if possible, to stain the pride of all glory in the creature; we are to preach not ourselves but Christ Jesus the Lord.
5. We must preach the Gospel depending on the operations of the Spirit to beat down the practical Arminianism of our natures ... Arminianism is the universal nature of mankind.
6. We ought to preach the Gospel discriminately, so as in the light of the Lord to define when Christ and salvation are effectually given, where, and in whose hands, the gift lies.
7. We must so preach the Gospel as to take special care that we distinguish the Spirit's work from the creature's acts, in the practical truths we preach.
8. We ought to preach the Gospel in the way of Christ's institution. The command runs thus, Preach the Word, be instant in season, out of season, &c., 2 Tim. iv. 2. But there is no command for offers.
9. We ought to preach the Gospel as it has a special promise of success.
10. We should preach the Gospel so that the Gospel may justify itself: for the Gospel being but of one piece of grace, through all parts of it, is fitted so to do.
11. We should preach the Gospel, because it is sure as to individual persons, or particular interests, me or thee. But offers are all indeterminate as to anybody and so indeed are fixed on nobody.
12. We should preach the Gospel as it is discovered to be an admirable contrivance of way and means to effect salvation.

13. We ought to preach the Gospel so as to exalt it higher than any unconverted man in the world can by his fleshly arm receive it, or carry it in the pulpit to offer it to others in such a way.
14. We should preach the Gospel singularly; so the greatest part of professing ministers do not preach it.
15. We ought to preach the Gospel in sincerity and truth, which if we do, it will not give that open offence to such as are taught by God the Spirit respecting his own work, which offers do.
16. We ought to preach the Gospel in the encouragements of it unto salvation. But offers are no encouragements to salvation. . . . Encouragements are God's operations of his grace.
17. We ought to preach the Gospel spiritually and discerningly, that the more our preaching is examined, cavilled at, despised, struck at and hated, the more it should discover . . . how sweetly it accords with the Spirit's work.
18. We ought to preach the Gospel so as Christ may see in it the travail of his soul and be satisfied.
19. We should preach the Gospel so as the ministers of Satan do not, nay, cannot; we should exalt free operations, which have from God an irresistible influence to overpower our corruptions, and free our wills of slavery and bondage to sin.
20. We are to preach the Gospel with confidence in Christ, and fear as to ourselves that we do not lay any stress upon the creature. Offers rob the Gospel of its properties, privileges and glory.

This doctrine of no offers of Christ developed quite naturally out of his extreme supralapsarianism. Indeed it was simply a logical deduction from it.

He faced the objection that the highly respected Independent Minister, Thomas Cole, had commended the practice of offering Christ to sinners in his *Discourse of Regeneration, Faith and Repentance* (1689), by stating that Cole could have been wrong just as John Calvin was not right in everything he said. To Hussey, any minister who claimed to believe in the sovereign grace of God but yet offered Christ to all was a "half-hearted Calvinist".

We have not discussed Hussey's doctrines of justification, assurance and atonement since they are virtually identical with those of Tobias Crisp which we have already discussed. The doctrines of eternal and virtual justification and the concept of assurance as the voice of the Spirit whispering "you are elect" were for Hussey the necessary corollaries of supralapsarian predestination and irresistible grace in conversion.

Like Crisp, when speaking of Christ's death, he tended to use terminology which made Christ as an actual sinner on the Cross, not as a Person to whom sins were only imputed.

It is probably true to say that Hussey's theology of grace is of such a type that it could only have been produced in the period of English history in which it actually was produced. It only becomes meaningful when it is seen as third generation Puritan Calvinistic doctrine, written when rationalism and latitudinarianism had made, and were making, inroads in all theological thinking.

By his doctrine of the God-Man, Hussey believed that he preserved the doctrines of the Person of Christ and the Trinity from all possibility of Socinian and Arian errors. He felt that his vision of the eternal Son of God, Who, in the everlasting covenant of grace assumed humanity, was such a Bible-based, God-given, picture of salvation, that it ruled out all human schemes whatever their origin. Through his doctrine of God's operations of grace but no offers of grace, resting firmly on eternal, absolute predestination, he believed that he saved the Gospel from the prevalent Arminianism of his age. And by his insistence that the Bible is a spiritual Book whose truth only "evangelical reason" can discover, he believed that he saved revealed religion from the errors of the Deists and followers of John Locke who used "natural reason".

Thus we see that Hussey's theology was a system of belief into which the spirit and temper of his age entered. Turning away from the various errors and heresies of his day, he adopted an extreme Reformed position, so extreme that it merits the title of "Hyper-Calvinism", since with its doctrine of no offers of grace and its supralapsarianism it rose well above (or sunk beneath) the theology of Calvin and of the orthodox Reformed Puritan divines.

Hussey died on 15th November, 1726, after moving from Cambridge to a London pastorate in Petticoat Lane in 1719. In forty-five years of preaching he had preached, according to his Diary, three thousand six hundred and seven sermons.

(d) *Criticism.* Only five hundred copies of the *Glory of Christ* were printed in 1706 and most of these were sold when Hussey wrote the preface to *God's Operation of Grace* in 1707. Despite the small printing, John Beart, Pastor of the Congregational Church at Bury St. Edmunds, could say that "the book of this learned man hath been the subject of much discourse". Beart's purpose in writing *A Vindication of the Eternal Law and the Everlasting Gospel* (1707) was to provide, from the High Calvinist standpoint, an answer to two false developments of Reformed theology, Baxterian, moderated Calvinism and the doctrines of Hussey. In the first part of the book he criticised the doctrines of Baxter and in the second part those of Hussey. The three doctrines of Hussey which he chose to attack were the God-Man Christology, the doctrine of eternal justification and the denial of the free offer of grace.

With regard to Hussey's view of the God-Man, Beart believed that it was a perversion of Goodwin's doctrine in that it tended to make the humanity of the Mediator exist in heaven before the actual Incarnation. In opposition to the doctrine of eternal justification and its corollary that justification by faith is merely a persuasion that one is already justified, Beart advocated the doctrine of virtual justification in the resurrection of Christ and a valid justification of the sinner through grace and by faith. Of the latter he wrote that "there is, at, or upon believing, some true and real act of God toward the soul, which is not merely a manifestation of what was done before, but is truly justification".[34] Beart also held that "the Free Tender of Christ is the soul's warrant for receiving him". He felt that "there must be a Warrant in the *Word* as well as in the *heart*".[35] In his doctrines of justification and the free tender of Christ, Beart was repeating what men like Ames, Owen and Goodwin had often said in the previous century.

(e) *The influence of Hussey's theology.* We know of three ministers upon whom Hussey had a direct doctrinal influence. One was Samuel Stockell, to whom we have already made reference in Chapter II, and who developed Hussey's God-

Man Christology as well as propagating the "no offers of grace" theology. We shall make reference to Stockell's influence in the concluding chapter. Another was William Bentley, minister of the Congregational Church which met in Crispin Street, Southwark, in the 1730s. He wrote an account of the last dying moments of Hussey.[36] The third was John Skepp whose doctrine of conversion we shall study in the rest of this chapter.

JOHN SKEPP

In his Diary, Hussey wrote in three places the following note on John Skepp:

> John Skep, of Little Wilburn, Miller, he rent himself off at last from the Church (in Cambridge) and turned Anabaptist preacher, yet was a Lad converted throughly to Christ under my Preaching, spake on Soul-work clearly and was admitted into the Church with much Satisfaction. After all this has repented of his sin and is returned, and Liberty given him to Preach as a Gifted Brother at Wittelsea. And last of all is dismissed to be the Pastor of an Anabaptist Church in London.

This Church was the Particular Baptist Church which met in Curriers' Hall, Cripplegate.[37] He only wrote one book: *Divine Energy or the Operations of the Spirit of God upon the soul of man in his effectual calling and conversion, stated, proved, and vindicated . . . being an antidote against the Pelagian error.* It was printed posthumously in 1722. The title and the contents bear witness to the influence of Hussey and repeat the excessive emphasis on irresistible grace found in *God's Operations of Grace.* We shall consider Skepp's doctrine of conversion under three headings.

(a) *The true nature of conversion.* Before providing the reader with his own view of conversion, Skepp gave five examples of the way in which people confused true conversion with similar, yet different, phenomena. First, some confused it with a mere improvement in Biblical knowledge. Secondly, others confused it with the obvious efforts of certain individuals to live a sober, religious life. Thirdly, some identified it with the sudden change of opinions in one who, after being an opponent of the Christian faith, becomes its defender. Fourthly, others equated it with a sudden change from loose morality to the observance of strict religious duties. Finally, many believed that if a person was brought up in a Christian family he was automatically a Christian.

Realising that some would accuse him of making the Christian life too difficult, Skepp felt obliged to explain why it was, in his opinion, no longer possible in the 1720s to accept a person into Church membership merely on the ground that the person confessed that Jesus was the Messiah, as the Apostles seem to have done. Such a brief confession, he reasoned, was quite sufficient in the early days of the Church but since the Church in the eighteenth century was surrounded and invaded by many erroneous systems of theology, most of which taught that Jesus was the Messiah, it was no longer a sure basis from which to ascertain genuine Christian grace and discipleship, despite what the great John Locke had said. Skepp believed that the words of Christ in Luke 6. 44, concerning the tree bearing fruit, had a primary reference not to the Christian producing good works for God's glory but to the belief in sound, Biblical doctrines.[38].

(*b*) *The inability of human power to convert sinners.* Skepp held that the powers of human rhetoric and persuasion could make no contribution whatsoever to the divine process of conversion. So he attacked "Pelagian" preachers[39] who used moral suasion and he defined the latter thus:

Moral suasion is an endeavour, by proper methods and arguments to persuade a man, in a natural unrenewed state, not only to break off and forsake his evil courses of sin and folly, but also closely to adhere unto the practice of moral and religious duties; or to put forth his power, and use his utmost endeavour to convert himself, and become a new man, and to live according to the strict rules of the Gospel, which require repentance toward God and faith in our Lord Jesus Christ, with constant perseverance therein.[40]

Whilst he admitted that God does make use of some exhortations in the Scriptures, he added that "He always superadds the efficacious power of His Spirit . . . to quicken and renew those souls for whom He has an eternal purpose of love and grace".⁴¹ His opinion was that the Gospel itself was, strictly speaking, "nothing but the blessed news and glad tidings of a salvation that is all of grace" and the promises, encouragements and reproofs connected with it were but "a sort of adjuncts or necessary concomitants attending the ministry of the Word".⁴²

It was so easy, he believed, in pressing men to repent to fall into Arminian discourse and to address the sinner as though he were able to save himself. He felt that if preachers were to realise the great obstacles which stand in the way of a sinner's conversion to God, they would not fall into the serious error of speaking like the Pelagians and Arminians. Skepp believed that man possessed no powers to accept the grace of God because by the fall of Adam the whole race had been rendered spiritually impotent. Also within human beings he saw a deep-seated natural rebellion against God and His mercy. The power of sin and Satan ruled supreme in the human heart. No human rhetoric could possibly move such obstacles. Divine power alone could deal with sin and Satan.

In his fear that the preacher was becoming an Arminian if he pressed men to repent and turn to Christ, Skepp displayed the same frame of mind as Hussey had expressed. He made sure that he completely avoided Arminian tendencies and, in doing so, lost sight of the fact that the Bible provides many examples of prophets and preachers who call men to turn to God without first giving long explanations as to the necessary work of the Spirit in the heart, mind and will.

(c) *The Spirit's energy in conversion.* Skepp emphasised that an elect person is passive in regeneration and also tended to refer to conversion as a whole as an act of God in which the elect soul is passive. He described the preparatory work of the Spirit in the following way:

> The Spirit first giveth the soul a repeated survey of its past and present sinful life. Secondly, as a Spirit of conviction, He giveth the soul an astonishing conviction and sight of his own vileness, and guiltiness before God, and wrath and vengeance he has deserved. Thirdly, He giveth the soul a humbling view of the corruption and uncleanness of his nature, as to the filth, depravity, perverseness, and deceit therein, all which make up

the plague of the heart. Fourthly, He convinceth that soul of its real impotency and disability to perform that which is truly and spiritually good and acceptable before God. Fifthly, He convinceth the soul of the real need and necessity of saving faith in Christ and of the pernicious effects and damnable nature of the sin of unbelief.[43]

Next the Spirit leads the soul into "a real, spiritual, vital union to Christ" Who is "the head and root of all spiritual life". This is followed by regeneration, the creation of a new nature within the soul of an elect person. From the moment of this new birth, all good works, thoughts and intentions pleasing to God, proceed from the inspiration of the indwelling Holy Spirit.

To illustrate true conversion Skepp made reference to the experience of Augustine of Hippo and of Thomas Goodwin.[44] He believed that what happened to them was true regeneration and true conversion. His book ends with a call to his hearers who did not find the signs of true conversion in their hearts to pray God to enlighten and to move them towards Himself, since there was nothing else they could do. Whilst the orthodox Puritans of the seventeenth century would have agreed with most of what Skepp had to say they would have pointed out that as surely as the Bible teaches the sovereignty of God's grace in conversion it also teaches that the preacher must call his hearers to faith in Christ and that he must not try to reconcile two Biblical doctrines which are portrayed as being "in tension" in the Bible.

(*d*) *The influence of Skepp.* As a preacher and writer, Skepp's influence was felt in Particular Baptist circles both in London and in Cambridgeshire. He must bear much of the responsibility for the introduction of Hussey's "no offers of grace" theology to Particular Baptists. Also his influence was continued after his death by Mrs. Ann Dutton who was once a member of his London Church and who became a prolific writer on religious topics. We shall say more about Mrs. Dutton and Skepp's influence on Baptists in later chapters. Skepp stands, as it were, in the history of dogma, as the connecting link between Hussey's theology and the

NO OFFERS OF GRACE

Hyper-Calvinism of many Particular Baptists throughout the eighteenth century.

[1] Cf. R. Davis, *Truth and Innocency Vindicated* . . ., pp. 5 ff.
[2] Hussey, *Glory of Christ*, p. 209.
[3] See A. G. Matthews, *Diary of a Cambridge Minister*, for a brief sketch of his life.
[4] Whitaker was educated at Magdalene College. In April, 1672, he was licensed as a Presbyterian preacher in Fordingbridge.
[5] Hussey, *op. cit.*, pp. 120 ff.
[6] The actual diary in which Hussey kept a record of his sermons and of church activities is now in the possession of Emmanuel Congregational Church, Cambridge. A typescript of part of it was kindly loaned to me by Mr. A. Smith on behalf of the deacons. Cf. Appendix I.
[7] Stephen Scandrett (1631-1706) was ejected from Trinity College, Oxford. Robert Billio (1623-1695) was also an ejected minister, whilst John King (1668-1746) had studied under Charles Morton and had opposed R. Davis.
[8] Hussey, *op. cit.*, p. 123.
[9] *Ibid*, p. 8.
[10] *Ibid*, p. 105.
[11] *Ibid*, p. 6.
[12] *Ibid*, p. 8.
[13] *Ibid*, pp. 111 ff.
[14] See Chapter I.
[15] Hussey, *Glory of Christ*, p. 536.
[16] Both are reprinted in the folio edition of his *Works* (1682-1704) and in the 1861-1865 edition (edited by John C. Miller) of his *Works*.
[17] Hussey, *op. cit.*, Preface, p. v.
[18] Hussey, *God's Operations* . . . (1707), Preface.
[19] Goodwin, *Works* (ed. Miller), Vol. IV, p. 490.
[20] *Ibid*, p. 503.
[21] *Ibid*, p. 488.
[22] Hussey, *Glory of Christ*, p. 90.
[23] *Ibid*, p. 75.
[24] *Ibid*, p. 108.
[25] *Ibid*, p. 86.
[26] *Ibid*, p. 161.
[27] *Ibid*, p. 127.
[28] *Ibid*, p. 797.
[29] *God's Operations of Grace* (1792 edition), p. 37.
[30] *Ibid*, p. 84.
[31] *Ibid*, p. 91.
[32] *Ibid*, p. 171.
[33] *Ibid*, pp. 203 ff.
[34] Beart, *Vindication* . . ., Part II, p. 26.
[35] *Ibid*, p. 50.
[36] Bentley, *The Lord the helper of his people: with the last dying words of* . . . *J. H.* (1733).
[37] For a brief history of this Church see W. Wilson, *History and Antiquities of Dissenting Churches* . . . *in London*, Vol. II, pp. 559 ff.

[38] Skepp, *Divine Energy...*, p. 36. This and all other references are to the 1851 edition.
[39] That is preachers who believed that unregenerate sinners had power to accept without divine aid the grace of God. For the original heresy of Pelagius see J. N. D. Kelly, *Early Christian Doctrines*, pp. 357 ff.
[40] Skepp, *op. cit.*, p. 58.
[41] *Ibid*, p. 61.
[42] *Ibid*, p. 61.
[43] *Ibid*, p. 211.
[44] *Ibid*, pp. 231 ff. for Augustine and pp. 233 ff. for Goodwin.

PART THREE

THE PROPAGATION OF HYPER-CALVINISM

CHAPTER V

THREE THEOLOGIANS

Synopsis: 1. The influence of Richard Davis. 2. Lewis Wayman. 3. John Gill. 4. John Brine.

It is our task in this chapter to describe the careers of the three men whom we have chosen as examples, in their theological thinking, of Hyper-Calvinism. They were Lewis Wayman, a Congregational minister, John Gill and John Brine, both Baptist ministers. Since all three, directly or indirectly, were connected with Richard Davis, we shall first, by way of introduction, make brief reference to his evangelistic and doctrinal influence.

THE INFLUENCE OF RICHARD DAVIS

Until Joseph Hussey's arguments against the offer of the grace of Christ to hearers of the Gospel became known, Davis freely offered Christ to men just as Tobias Crisp and Thomas Cole had done. In his autobiography Joseph Perry, a convert of Davis, testified to the open invitation to sinners in the preaching of Davis.

> I remember when he used to speak to sinners (for then I did listen in particular) he would exhort with great earnestness poor sinners to come to Christ, sinners as they were, and believe on him at the word of command: "This is the command of God that you believe on his Son", I John 3. 23, and not stand in dispute whether or not thou art worthy or not worthy, elected or not elected, this being a secret not for us to pry into, but as sinners we must come to Christ and believe on him or be damned.[1]

However, as John Gill pointed out in his preface to the seventh edition of the *Hymns* of Richard Davis,[2] the latter did change his mind on this matter in the closing years of his life. Thus it is very probable that many of his converts and followers also adopted Hussey's belief that the doctrines of grace should only be preached not offered.

Though they had converts in many places, Davis and his helpers only established six Churches. These were at Welling-

A REFUTATION

OF

ARMINIAN PRINCIPLES,

Delivered in a Pamphlet, intitled, the

MODERN QUESTION

Concerning

Repentance *and* Faith, *examined with Candour,* &c.

In a LETTER to a FRIEND.

By *JOHN BRINE.*

LONDON:

Printed for, and Sold by A. Ward, at the *King's-Arms* in *Little-Britain,* MDCCXLIII.

(Price Six-Pence.)

THREE THEOLOGIANS 95

borough (1691), Thorpe Waterville (1694), and Ringstead (1714) in Northamptonshire, Needingworth (1693) and Kimbolton (1693) in Huntingdonshire, and Guyhurn in Cambridgeshire.[3] They were also closely associated with the formation of the Independent Church at Southill in Bedfordshire.[4] These Churches formed centres from which the influence of Davis, tempered by Hussey's views on preaching, continued to flow. It is to the life and career of a pastor of one of these Churches that we now turn.

Lewis Wayman[5]

Lewis Wayman was a knacker and collar-maker by trade, working for those who owned horses. As a youth he became a member of the Rothwell Church during the period when Richard Davis was its pastor. When it was noticed that he had a gift for preaching, he was heard by the Church and then given permission to become an itinerant minister. One of the places at which he preached was Kimbolton, which, as we have seen, had intimate connections with Rothwell. After the death of its second minister, Richard Bailey, in 1714, Wayman was one of the supplies who were invited to fill the pulpit. In the Kimbolton Church book the following entry is found, dated 23rd June, 1717:

> It was agreed on by the Church non contridicting, that we desier brother Wayman to continue amongst us and that to go forwards in order to be our pastor, and we appoynt our breathren in town to discors and conclude with brother Wayman what may be needfull thereunto about his settlement amongst us and his dismission to us.

On 13th October, 1717, the letter from Rothwell agreeing to release Wayman from his membership was read to the Kimbolton Church, but it was not until 15th January, 1718, that Wayman was ordained and set apart to the office of pastor. Messengers from Rothwell, Kettering, Wellingborough, Higham Ferrers, Ringstead and Thorpe Waterville were present at this ceremony. It is unlikely that Wayman continued to make harnesses and collars for horses after his ordination since in a sermon a few years later he said:

There is nothing more plain in Scripture than this, that those whom God hath set apart to the work of the ministry are exempted from other worldly trades and callings.[6]

He remained pastor of the Church for forty-six years until his death in March, 1764.

Though he published only two tracts and a few funeral sermons, it is possible to be fairly accurate in estimating what were the major theological influences in his thinking. As a member of the Rothwell Church, he was obviously nurtured in a High Calvinism which showed some sympathy towards the doctrinal antinomianism of Tobias Crisp. Here also he was probably introduced to the writings of John Owen and Thomas Goodwin to which he made reference in his tracts. Yet his admiration for Goodwin seems to have surpassed that for Owen. And the way in which he quoted from and defended the two influential books of Joseph Hussey shows that he had carefully absorbed them and accepted the essentials of the dogma. Indeed, Hussey seems to have been highly respected by the Kimbolton Church since he preached there on several occasions, including the funeral sermon for Richard Bailey.[7]

Wayman's Hyper-Calvinism is clearly reflected in the part he took in the controversy concerning "the modern question" which we shall discuss in Chapter VII. It is because of the important part that he had in this controversy that we have included him in this study together with the more prolific writers, Gill and Brine.

JOHN GILL[8]

John Gill was born in 1697. His parents were zealous Nonconformists who had been members of the Great Meeting (now Toller Meeting) in Kettering but were attending, at the time of his birth, the Little Meeting (now Fuller Meeting) which had been formed in 1696 by a secession from the Great Meeting. The Little Meeting was a Baptist Church. Its first minister, William Wallis, had been the elder who administered adult baptism in the parent Church. He was succeeded by his son in 1713 and it is interesting to note that

Edward Gill, the father of John Gill, was appointed a deacon in the Church sometime before 1713.

As soon as he was old enough, John was sent to the local grammar school where he quickly gained a basic knowledge of grammar, Latin and Greek. In 1708, the schoolmaster, who was an Anglican, decided to make daily attendance at the Parish Church compulsory for his boys. As the Gill family could not agree to this imposition, John, now a lad of eleven years, had to leave school. Some neighbouring ministers tried to find some way to enable him to continue his education but their efforts were without success. The possibility remains, however, that he did spend a brief period in the home of Richard Davis at Rothwell, which had to end because of the illness of Davis.[9] The young Gill had a thirst for knowledge and allowed nothing to stand in his way. He continued his studies privately, seeking to master his knowledge of Latin and Greek, and extending his studies to cover logic, rhetoric, moral philosophy and Hebrew. Also he read the Latin works of various continental divines from which he was later to quote liberally.

On the first day of November, 1716, he made a public profession of faith to the congregation at the Little Meeting, and afterwards was baptised by Thomas Wallis. Following the advice of some London friends he moved soon afterwards to Higham Ferrers in order to live with John Davis, a Welshman,[10] who had recently arrived there to be the minister of the newly-formed Baptist Church. The intention was that Gill should continue his studies with the help of Davis and also preach in the neighbouring villages. This he did and also married Elizabeth Negus, a member of the Church.

In 1719 Gill accepted a call to become the minister of the Particular Baptist Church which met at Horsleydown, Southwark, in succession to Benjamin Stinton. Due to various troubles in the Church,[11] the ordination ceremony was delayed until March 22nd, 1720. Significantly, one of the ministers who took part in the ceremony was John Skepp. Gill had a great respect for John Skepp and in his preface to the second edition of *Divine Energy* he wrote: "The worthy author . . .

was personally and intimately known by me and his memory precious to me". After Skepp's death in 1721, Gill purchased most of his Hebrew and Rabbinical books and made great use of them both in his commentary on the Old Testament and in his polemical treatises.

He remained pastor of the Church until he died in 1771. Throughout these long years he was in constant demand as a preacher at ordinations and funerals. From 1729 to 1756 he preached at the Wednesday Lecture in Great Eastcheap and several of his books had their origin as lectures here. Also he was chosen as one of the nine lecturers who gave the Lime Street Lectures in 1730-1731. His subject was "The Resurrection of the Dead".

He saw himself not only as a pastor and casuist but also as a defender of what he believed was the Reformed faith. This made him an ardent controversialist. Because of the progress of heterodox views of the Trinity and the Person of Christ he wrote *The Doctrine of the Trinity stated and vindicated* (1731). In answer to the charges of Abraham Taylor and Job Burt[12] that the doctrine of eternal justification caused antinomianism he wrote *The Doctrine of God's Everlasting Love to His Elect and their Eternal Union to Christ* (1732), *Truth Defended* (1736), and *The Necessity of Good Works unto Salvation considered* (1739). When John Wesley attacked both the doctrine of absolute predestination and the doctrine of the final perseverance of the saints, Gill replied with *The Doctrine of Predestination Stated and set in Scripture-light* (1752), and *The Doctrine of the Saints Final Perseverance Asserted and Vindicated* (1752). His four-volume *The Cause of God and Truth* (1734-1738) was written to answer the *Discourse on Election* by Dr. Daniel Whitby which had been republished in 1735. Gill was also a staunch Baptist and defended Baptist principles against many critics. His three-volume *Body of Divinity*, published at the end of his life, contained the substance of the sermons he had preached to his congregation.

Gill's theological sympathies are reflected in his connection with the publication of several books. He wrote a preface to the *Hymns* of Richard Davis in 1748, edited Skepp's *Divine Energy* in 1751, as well as Crisp's *Works* in 1755, and together with John Brine, signed the prefatory "epistle to the reader" of the *Oeconomy of the Covenants* by Herman Witsius in 1763.

When they become adults some men despise and forget the religious teaching to which, as boys, they were subjected. This was true of many men in the early years of the eighteenth century as they departed from the orthodox Calvinism of their youth to adopt Arminian principles. But this did not happen to John Gill. He spent his whole life learning more about and defending the teaching which, as a young man, he had learned in Northamptonshire. The High Calvinism of Richard Davis, hardened by controversy with Baxterianism and Arminianism, modified through the assimilation of Crispian doctrines, and severely conditioned by the influence of Hussey's "no offers of grace" theology, was the theological environment in which Gill was nurtured. Of Crisp and Hussey he wrote:

> They were both, in their day and generation, men of great piety and learning, of long standing and much usefulness in the Church of Christ, whose name and memory will be dear and precious to the saints when this writer (Job Burt) and his pamphlet will be remembered no more.[13]

He deepened this theology through the study of certain continental and English High Calvinists and was, no doubt, confirmed in his views through his friendship with John Skepp.

The footnotes in his books reveal that throughout his life he was an avid and wide reader. There are many quotations from Rabbinical, patristic, philosophical and even scientific books.[14] The writers whom he quoted approvingly were few and were all Reformed divines with the exception of Augustine. They included Jacobus Altingius (1583-1644), professor at Amsterdam; Johannes Cocceius (1613-1669), the famous federal theologian;[15] Johannes Henricus Heideggerus (1633-1698), professor at Zurich; Johannes Hoornbeck (1617-1666), professor at Leyden; Johannes Maccovius (1588-1644), professor at Franeker; Marcus F. Wendelinus (1584-1652), a leading Reformed scholastic theologian; Johannes Wollebius (1586-1629), professor at Basel; Herman Witsius (1636-1708),

(1636-1708), a federal theologian; and the British divines, William Ames, William Pemble, Samuel Rutherford, William Twisse, Thomas Goodwin and John Owen.

Gill had two intimate friends, J. C. Ryland, a Baptist minister, and Augustus Toplady, an Anglican clergyman. So great was the latter's admiration for Gill that he wrote: "While true religion and sound learning have a single friend in the British Empire, the works and name of *Gill* will be precious and revered".[16]

JOHN BRINE[17]

Into a poor, godly home in Kettering John Brine was born in 1703. At a very young age he had to begin work to help his family and so had no chance of attending a school. Though he must have heard the Gospel many times both from his father, who was a member of the Little Meeting, and from others, it was under the preaching of John Gill, who was six years his senior, that he was actually converted. Many years later, Gill referred to him as among "the firstfruits" of his ministry.[18] Brine was baptised by Thomas Wallis and admitted into Church membership. On the one remaining page of the Church record book for this period, the signature of Brine appears, written presumably when he joined the Church. This conversion experience served not only to give him a desire for the things of God, but also a zeal to acquire a working knowledge of the ancient languages and a better literary taste. In these early days of academic study, John Gill and Thomas Wallis acted as his teachers. It did not take the Church long to realise that Brine had the necessary gifts and calling to be a preacher. Accordingly, the Church called him into the ministry of the Word just as previously it had called Gill. For a few years he served as an itinerant minister in the neighbouring villages and proved acceptable. During this period he came into contact with John Moore, minister of the Nonconformist Church which met in College Lane, Northampton, and he married his youngest daughter, Anne.[19]

John Moore had been set apart as pastor of the Northampton Church in December, 1700, when messengers from the

Rothwell Church were present. Earlier Richard Davis himself had been present as a witness at the formation of the Church in 1697, and later the Rothwell Church gave a gift towards the erection of a Meeting House.[20] Thus the influence of Davis came to Brine through Gill and Moore. To Moore also, Brine owed both his copy of Hutter's Hebrew Bible and the introduction to his first pastorate. In the oldest minute book of the Church now meeting in Queen's Road, Coventry, there is a record of payments made to John Moore for preaching there in 1725. The church to which Moore preached was a Particular Baptist Church and it met in a little square brick building in Will Raton's yard, in Jordan Well, Coventry. A year later Brine preached here and by October, 1726, he had been chosen as pastor.[21] In February, 1727, he was taken into full membership of the Church and commenced his pastoral duties. He remained here until July 27th, 1729, when he moved to London to become pastor of the congregation which met in Curriers' Hall, Cripplegate, and whose pastor had once been John Skepp who died in 1721.

With John Gill, Brine "cultivated a particular friendship, which was strengthened by a congeniality of views on religious subjects".[22] He also read widely to furnish himself with material in order to defend the doctrines he had learned as a youth in Kettering. He saw the duties of the ministry as twofold. The first was "the defence of the principles of . . . revelation" and the second was the necessity of convincing church-goers of their "lukewarmness, indifferency and sad declension".[23] Thus, apart from his pastoral duties he sought to defend his faith against Deism,[24] Arianism[25] and Baxterianism.[26]

The authorities whom Brine quoted approvingly were virtually the same as those quoted by Gill. Witsius, Pemble and Goodwin were his particular favourites. Whilst he regarded Hussey as a "great and learned man", he did not accept everything that he had written uncritically. He disagreed with Hussey's distinction between "everlasting" and "eternal".[27] But he did accept Hussey's belief that it is wrong to offer the grace of Christ to all.

In London, Brine took an active part in the affairs of the Particular Baptist denomination and preached at many ordination and funeral services. When John Gill retired from the Great Eastcheap Lecture in 1756, Brine was one of the ministers chosen to continue the Lecture. Also he preached regularly at the Sunday evening Lecture at Devonshire Square, in the Meeting House of the Particular Baptist Church. After an illness he died on 21st February, 1765, and like Gill, was buried in Bunhill Fields.

[1] From the *Life and miraculous conversion from Popery of Joseph Perry*, quoted by Glass, *op. cit.*, pp. 154 ff., and by the *Gospel Standard* in July, 1853.
[2] "Whereas the phrase of *offering Christ and Grace* is sometimes used in these Hymns, which may be offensive to some persons; and which the worthy author was led to the use of, partly thro' custom, it not having been objected to, and partly thro' his affectionate concern and zeal for gaining upon souls, and encouraging them to come to Christ; I can affirm upon good and sufficient Testimony, that Mr. Davis, before his death, changed his mind in this matter, and disused the phrase as being improper, and as being too bold and free, for a minister of Christ to make use of . . . ."
[3] Glass, *op. cit.*, Chapter 9.
[4] Cf. H. G. Tibbutt, "New Light on Northamptonshire Nonconformist History", *Northamptonshire Past and Present*, IV (1966-1967), pp. 61 ff.
[5] Not a lot is known about Wayman. The following facts are gleaned from two sources: (i) "The first Church book of the Kimbolton Independent Church", in typescript in Dr. Williams's Library, copied by H. G. Tibbutt. (ii) "The Nonconformist Churches at Hail-Weston, St. Neots, etc." in five volumes of MS. also in Dr. Williams's Library and by Joseph Rix.
[6] Quoted by Rix, Vol. 5, p. 1.
[7] This information is to be found in the Diary of Hussey. The funeral sermon was preached on 23rd June, 1714.
[8] Some of the following detail is taken from J. Rippon, *Brief Memoir of the Life and Writings of . . . John Gill* (1838).
[9] Davis had been a schoolmaster in London before 1689. In his preface to the *Hymns* of Davis, Gill wrote: "I had the honour in my youth of knowing him; his memory has always been precious to me, partly on account of his great regard both for my Education, for which he was heartily concerned, and also for my spiritual and eternal welfare". We know that Davis took young men into his home as students from the following statement: "In order to perpetuate this schism, Davis breeds up young men in his house", in the anonymous *Doctrine and Discipline of Mr. Richard Davis of Rothwell* (1700), p. 22.
[10] John Davis does not seem to have been a relative of Richard Davis. Yet he was certainly of similar religious convictions. He moved from Higham Ferrers to Cambridge after 1721 to become pastor of a Baptist Church whose origin was in a secession from the Church of which Hussey

was pastor until 1719. Cf. B. Nutter, *The Story of the Cambridge Baptists*, p. 83.
[11] Cf. B. R. White, "Thomas Crosby, Baptist Historian", *B.Q.* XXI (October, 1965), for the background to these troubles.
[12] Taylor made the charge in one of his lectures at Lime Street and also printed it in his lecture when it was published in 1732 with the other lectures in *Defense of some important doctrines*. Burt wrote *Some doctrines in the supralapsarian scheme examined* (1736).
[13] Gill, *Truth Defended*, in *Sermons and Tracts*, Vol. II, p. 81.
[14] *E.g.* William Whiston, *A New Theory of the Earth* (1696).
[15] Cf. "Cocceius, Johannes and his school", *New Schaff-Herzog Encyclopedia of Religious Knowledge*, Vol. III.
[16] Rippon, *op. cit.*, p. 140.
[17] For a brief sketch of Brine's life see Wilson, *op. cit.*, Vol. II, pp. 574 ff.
[18] Gill, *Sermons and Tracts*, Vol. I, p. 591.
[19] For the history of the Church see E. A. Payne, *College Street Church, Northampton, 1697-1947*. Moore was a Yorkshireman who in the 1690s engaged in evangelism with William Mitchell and David Crosley in the Pennines.
[20] For the relations between Rothwell and Northampton see Glass, *op. cit.*, pp. 129 ff.
[21] Cf. I. Morris, *Three Hundred Years of Baptist Life in Coventry*, pp. 12 ff.
[22] Wilson, *op. cit.*, Vol. II, p. 575.
[23] Preface to *Treatise on various subjects* (1750).
[24] *E.g.* he wrote against Dodwell in *The Christian Religion not destitute of Arguments sufficient to support it* (1746).
[25] *E.g.* he wrote against Taylor of Norwich in *The True Sense of Attonement for Sin* (1752).
[26] *E.g.* he wrote against Watts in *The Certain Efficacy of the Death of Christ* (1743).
[27] *Proper Eternity of the Divine Decrees* (1754), pp. 2 ff.

CHAPTER VI

GOD, HIS DECREES AND COVENANTS

Synopsis: 1. The Sources of the knowledge of God: (*a*) Natural Religion; (*b*) Divine Revelation. 2. The Internal Acts of God: (*a*) Predestination; (*b*) Eternal Union; (*c*) Eternal Adoption; (*d*) Eternal Justification. 3. The Covenant of Grace. 4. The Covenant of Works. 5. Calvin and Hyper-Calvinism.

Concerning the Augustan Age in which the authors we are studying lived and worked, Carl L. Becker has written: "What we have to realise is that in those years God was on trial".[1] We may agree with Becker as the doctrine of God is the foundation of all theology and was certainly a subject of much discussion in the first half of the eighteenth century. It is against this background of rational enquiry that we must set the Hyper-Calvinist doctrine of God.

THE SOURCES OF THE KNOWLEDGE OF GOD

(*a*) *Natural Religion.* The question as to what positive contribution the study of nature could make to the knowledge of God was a vital question to be faced in an age when Deism was popular. Brine asserted that the careful study of nature could, and did, lead men not merely into a belief in the existence of an eternal Being, the Creator of the universe, but also into a belief in His unity, His spirituality, His simplicity, His omnipresence, omniscience, omnipotence and His immutability. He sought to prove this assertion with quotations from such writers as Cicero, Pythagoras, Plato and Seneca.[2] Yet he was careful to add that this knowledge, when compared with divine revelation, was partial and deficient. "That there is a God may be known by the light of nature", wrote John Gill, "but who and what he is, men destitute of divine revelation have been at a loss about."[3] In a brief reference to the subject Wayman wrote:

God has written one book for reason to read in, another for faith; the creatures discover to reason, now eclipsed, the eternal power and godhead; but God's glories are written in the face of Jesus Christ as mediator and saviour, and there it is that the saved of the Lord read his glories and shall be reading of them to all eternity.[4]

It was felt that the religion of nature did not teach men how to worship God aright and could offer no help to troubled consciences. However, had man not sinned, the light of nature would have been sufficient to teach him, in that state of perfection, all that he needed to know about God. But the fact was clear that the human race was fallen and without any resources to have fellowship with God. It was, wrote Brine, only "in the glass of the Christian revelation (that) we have presented to our view truths more sublime, more noble, and far more glorious than our reason could ever have thought of; nay, than reason, in a state of perfection, could have discovered".[5]

Nevertheless, as Brine pointed out in his reply to James Foster, the Arian, reason is not to be abandoned by those who believe in the superiority of divine revelation. The purpose of reason is to judge the sense of revelation. It has to consider the import of the language of Scripture, to compare one part of revelation with another, and to discern when metaphor, allegory and analogy are being used by the inspired writers. Also he held that:

Reason is to infer conclusions from premises which revelation delivers. And this may be done with certainty provided we proceed carefully in considering the true sense of the propositions wherein some truths are contained, from which other truths are evidently deducible.[6]

This hermaneutical principle was often used by the Hyper-Calvinists, especially in their distinctive additions to High Calvinism.

(b) *Divine Revelation.* The enquiring minds of the eighteenth century claimed to accept nothing without sufficient proof. Therefore those who regarded the Bible as the inerrant word of God felt obliged to give good reasons for their belief. John Gill gave seven reasons why he believed the Bible to be of divine origin.[7] We may summarise these as follows:

106   HYPER-CALVINISM

1. The Bible contains nothing unworthy of God. Its books contain no falsehood or contradiction and its contents are so holy and divine that no human author could possibly have written them, as is seen in the fact that the prophecies of the Old Testament are so perfectly fulfilled in the New Testament.
2. The Bible is written in such an authoritative style and manner. The majestic language of Isaiah, the speeches of Jehovah in the book of Job, and the beautiful words of the Psalms reveal a divine author.
3. The message and truth of the Bible is one, but the authors are many and of varied type. The fact that all these authors are in agreement means that they were all penmen of the Holy Spirit.
4. The reading and hearing of the Scriptures have had a marvellous effect on the lives of men and women. Under the influence of the Bible many people have turned from wickedness to lead a godly life.
5. Miracles can only be performed by God. The Bible contains the accounts of many miracles performed by the power of God. Thus the Bible must be God's book.
6. Wicked and perverse men have opposed the printing and distribution of the Bible. They would not have adopted this attitude had it not been completely opposed to *their* way of life.
7. Many of the books of the Bible are very old and as Tertullian once said, "That which is most ancient is most true".

Gill also had definite views about the inspiration of the Bible. He held that its penmen wrote as they were directed, inspired and guided by the Holy Spirit. Not only the general message and substance of the Scriptures but the very words of the original languages also were suggested by the Holy Spirit to the human authors, and suggested in such a way as to correspond with the individual style of the author.

Though the nature of God revealed in the Bible cannot be fully comprehended by human minds, the duty of theologians is "to frame the best conceptions of him" and "to serve and worship him, honour and glorify him in the best manner".[8] Christ taught that God is a Spirit (John 4. 22-24) and this means, thought Gill, that God, as the highest form of Spirit is immaterial, incorruptible, immortal, invisible, and endowed with the highest form of understanding, will and affections. He is eternal and immutable in His nature and purposes, an infinite being. Also He is omniscient, omnipotent, omnipresent, wise, sovereign in all things, merciful, loving, good, holy, hateful towards sin, faithful, self-sufficient and blessed. The Bible revealed that God was One in Three:

> That there is a God, and that there is but one God, who is a Being possessed of all divine perfections, may be known by the light of nature: but that there is a Trinity of persons in the Godhead, who are distinct, though not divided from each other, is what natural reason could never have discovered.[9]

This plurality in the Godhead is revealed in Scripture in three ways. First, plural names and epithets are used of God; *e.g.* "Elohim" in Genesis 1. 1. Secondly, plural expressions are used by God such as "Let us make man in our image", Genesis 1. 25, and "Who will go for us", Isaiah 6. 8. Thirdly, by the existence of the special angel of Jehovah in the Old Testament who, though distinct from Jehovah, speaks as Jehovah, as in Genesis 16. 7.[10]

Both Gill and Brine maintained that this plurality in the Godhead was not merely God appearing in various forms or having different names as taught in Sabellianism.[11] "The three in the Godhead are not barely three modes, but three distinct Persons in a different mode of subsisting."[12] The distinction of the Three Persons is as eternal as the eternity of God. Gill explained:

> It is in the personal relations, or distinctive relative properties which belong to each person, which distinguish them one from another; as paternity in the first Person, filiation in the second, and spiration in the third; or, more plainly, it is begetting, Psalm ii. 7, which peculiarly belongs to the first, and is never ascribed to the second or third; which distinguishes him from both, and gives him, with great propriety, the name of Father; and it is being begotten that is the personal relation, or relative property of the second Person; hence called "the only begotten of the Father", John i. 14, which distinguishes him from the first and the third, and gives him the name of Son; and the relative property or personal relation of the third Person is, that he is breathed by the first and second Persons; hence called, the breath of the Almighty, the breath of the mouth of Jehovah the Father, and the breath of the mouth of Christ the Lord, and which is never said of the other two Persons; and so distinguishes him from them and very pertinently gives him the name of Spirit.[13]

As Gill rightly observed: "the distinction of Persons in the Deity depends on the generation of the Son".[14] Though some learned theologians (*e.g.* Thomas Ridgley) might seek to explain the doctrine of the Trinity without this cardinal doctrine the fact remained, insisted Gill, that it is a necessary doctrine. Thus he defended the orthodox doctrine of the Trinity against both Socinian, Arian and Sabellian errors. Like John Brine he also denied that the soul of Christ existed in heaven and was joined to the God-Man before the Incarnation.[15] Indeed, in their doctrine of the Trinity the Hyper-Calvinists were entirely in harmony with the Catholic Creeds.

THE INTERNAL ACTS OF GOD

It was usual amongst Reformed theologians to distinguish between the internal and external acts of God, the latter having reference to what God has done and is doing in time, the former having reference to His eternal thoughts.[16] These eternal thoughts of God they divided into the personal and essential acts of God. Personal acts referred to the acts peculiar to each of the Three Persons, and essential acts to the common works and thoughts of all Three. The Hyper-Calvinists used these distinctions.

The decrees or counsels of God were regarded as part of the essential acts of God. "God is a Spirit, uncreated, infinite, operative and active; He must have been for ever active in Himself; His eternal mind must have always been employed."[17] Indeed, Brine criticised both Hussey and Stockell because their doctrine of the God-Man made the decrees of God to be temporal not eternal. He also tried to show that the favourite passage of these two men, Proverbs 8. 22ff., did teach the doctrine of the eternal generation of the Second Person of the Trinity.[18]

It was held that the decrees of God had reference to everything in the universe: the heavens (Psalm 148. 6), the earth (II Peter 3. 5), the seas (Job 38. 8ff.), the nations (Daniel 2), Israel (Genesis 15. 14), the Church, the lives of all people, and the life, death, resurrection of Jesus Christ. All the good in the world exists because of His effective decrees, whilst evil exists by His permissive decrees. Even the death of a sparrow is controlled by the purpose of God (Matthew 10. 29).

GOD, HIS DECREES AND COVENANTS 109

God's decrees are immanent acts since they are in Him, and remain and abide in Him until they are executed. They are free acts as no "outside power" influenced their constitution; and they are wise acts because God is wise. Also they are immutable, unalterable and effectual acts for God Himself is immutable.

(a) *Predestination*. The decrees of God concerning rational beings were called predestination. These decrees included not only the election of some individuals to salvation and the rejection of others, but also the predetermination of all things necessary to bring these decrees to fruition. God's first act of election was to choose Christ, the Mediator. In His eternal purposes God prepared a body and human nature for the Second Person of the Trinity. He purposed that the Son, as the God-Man, should be the Head of the elect and He had delight in His thoughts as He considered this: "Behold my servant, whom I uphold, mine Elect in whom my soul delighteth" (Isaiah 42. 1).

Gill argued that this predestination of individuals to eternal life and glory was not to be confused with the election of the nation of Israel to external privileges such as the possession of Canaan and the Temple cultus. Nor was election to be understood as having any reference to groups of people or to Churches. When Paul told the Thessalonians that they were the chosen and elect of God (I Thess. 1. 4), he meant that as individual Christians they were such.[19]

Also Gill argued that God is "the efficient cause" of election.[20] As a Sovereign Being, He has the right to choose whom He will and He has exerted this right. Those whom He has chosen He has placed in Christ, the Head of the elect, and Himself the "Elect One".

Though the Hyper-Calvinists preferred the supralapsarian view of predestination, they were not dogmatic on this question. Gill even wrote:

For my own part, I think that both (*i.e.* supralapsarianism and sublapsarianism) may be taken in; that in the decree of the end the ultimate end, the glory of God, for which He does all things men might be considered in the divine mind as creable, not yet created and fallen: and that in the decree of means, which, among other things, takes in the mediation of Christ, redemption by him and the sanctification of the Spirit, they might be considered as created, fallen and sinful, which these things imply; nor does this suppose separate acts and decrees in God, or any priority and posteriority in them; which in God are but one and together; but our finite minds are obliged to consider them one after another, not being able to take them in together, and at one.[21]

Brine believed that it was not a point over which "Calvinists" should disagree and argue,[22] and Gill reminded his readers that the greatest of all supralapsarians, William Twisse, had considered that the difference between the two views of predestination was only *apex logicus*, a logical point.

The decree of reprobation was considered as having two parts, preterition and pre-damnation. Preterition referred to God passing by some people as He looked upon the whole human race in His eternal thoughts and pre-damnation referred to God's condemnation of the future non-elect human beings to eternal perdition. "The sole, moving and impulsive cause of such a decree," wrote Gill, "(is) what Christ has expressed, 'Even so Father, for so it seemed good in thy sight'."[23] The decrees of God have their ultimate explanation in the good pleasure of God.

(*b*) *Eternal Union.*[24] It was believed that the elect are loved by God the Father, Son and Holy Spirit with an eternal love (Romans 8. 34). As the fruit of the Father's love the elect were eternally joined to Christ in "election-union" (Ephesians 1. 4). By the love of Christ to His Elect Bride, the Church, there was also "conjugal-union"; the secret act of betrothal was in eternity with the Holy Spirit as the Witness. In addition, there was the "federal-union" between Christ and the elect, since the covenant of grace was made, not with Christ as a single Person, but with Him as a representative Person, the Head of the elect. Finally, there was the "legal-union" between Christ and the elect, the bond of which is His Suretyship for them in the covenant of grace. This doctrine of eternal union was thus conceived as the first blessing of God's grace to the elect and as an immanent act of God.

(c) *Eternal Adoption*.[25] The Hyper-Calvinists held that, though all Christians are the children of God by faith in Christ, this sense of adoption, caused by the work of the Holy Spirit, is only an open manifestation in time of the eternal adoption of each elect person by God the Father in eternity. It is because the elect are already adopted that the Spirit of adoption is sent into their hearts. Adoption was therefore considered as an act of God's free grace from eternity, a logical consequence of eternal election and eternal union.

(d) *Eternal Justification*.[26] It was customary amongst some Reformed divines to divide justification into active and passive justification.[27] Active justification was thought of as that which took place in the immanent acts of God, whereas passive justification was held to be that act of God which terminates in time in the conscience of the elect believer. This way of treating justification was adopted by Gill and Brine who taught that the elect are eternally justified because of the sure nature of God's decrees of election and salvation. Brine defended this doctrine against Robert Bragge, one of the Lime Street lecturers, and Gill answered the objections of the learned Professor Turretine of Geneva.[28]

THE COVENANT OF GRACE[29]

We now turn to an examination of the eternal transactions and operations of God in Trinity. The Hyper-Calvinists distinguished the eternal counsel of God from the eternal covenant of grace and regarded the former as the foundation of the latter.

As Scripture states that the doctrines of the Gospel are the counsel of God (Acts 20. 27), it was their belief that these doctrines reflect the hidden wisdom of God. Thus there must have been some deliberation within the Godhead in eternity to formulate this counsel and wisdom. The words in Genesis 1. 25, "Let us make man in our image", show that deliberation took place about the creation and the nature of mankind. The eternal counsel of God which concerned itself with the salvation of men they called the "council of peace", Gill wrote:

Now the affair consulted about was not the salvation of men meerly; nor who should be the persons that should be saved with it; for both that was resolved on, and the persons fixed on who were to enjoy it in the decree of election, which stands firm and sure in the unalterable will of God; but who should be the Saviour, or be the author of this salvation; and a proper person for this work could never have been devised, found out, and pitched upon, by men and angels; this was the business of the great council.[80]

It was because of this eternal council that the covenant of grace came into being.

The covenant of grace was thought of as a compact or agreement made from eternity amongst the divine Persons, more especially between the Father and the Son, concerning the salvation of those already chosen in the decree of election. It was an agreement of the Trinity which presupposed the decrees of election and reprobation. [Thus it was in direct opposition to the doctrine (the "new method") of Saumur which placed the decree of election after the decree of universal redemption.] Whilst they believed that it was correct to call the covenant of grace the covenant of redemption, they believed it was wrong to divide the one covenant into two covenants as the followers of Richard Baxter did.

The Father, the First Person of the Trinity, took the initiative in the covenant. He proposed various conditions to the Second Person and these formed the *only* conditions of the covenant. They were that the Son, as the Messiah, should take full care of the elect souls whom the Father had chosen, and, because they were to be involved in the sin of Adam, that He should redeem them. This in turn meant that He must assume human nature, be born of a woman, perfectly obey the law of God, satisfy divine justice and bring in an everlasting righteousness for the elect.

The Father promised to the Son the full assistance of the Holy Spirit, the help of angels, and His own providential guidance in the everyday tasks of life. Also He promised the Son that in His human nature, as the Messiah, He would be exalted above all creation and be seated at God's right hand in triumph. Furthermore, He promised that the elect in the Messiah as their Head and Representative would be delivered

GOD, HIS DECREES AND COVENANTS

from sin and misery and then openly adopted, justified and glorified.

It was believed that the attitude of the Son in the covenant was expressed in Psalm 40. 7, "Lo, I come; in the volume of the book it is written of me, I delight to do thy will, O my God". He accepted the conditions put to Him by the Father: "Yea, thy law is within my heart". This acceptance of the Father's conditions meant that He became the Covenant-Head, Mediator, Surety and Testator of the covenant of grace.

The covenant conditions were put to him as the Representative of the elect and on their behalf He accepted them; it was this acceptance that made him their Covenant-Head. He agreed also to become the "one Mediator between God and man" (I Timothy 2. 5) which He was able to fufil perfectly since He was God and would become man. Part of the office of Mediator involved becoming the legal Surety of the elect (Hebrews 7. 22). Gill explained this concept of Christ as a Surety in the following way:

> Christ is in such sense a Surety civilians call an *exprommissor*, one that promises out and out, absolutely engages to pay another's debt; takes another's obligation, and transfers it to himself, and by this act dissolves the former obligation, and enters into a new one, which civilians call *novation*; so that the obligation no longer lies on the principal debtor, but he is set free, and the Surety is under the obligation, as if he was the principal debtor, or the guilty person. Now this sort of suretyship being most familiar, and coming nearest to Christ's suretyship, is made use of to express and explain it.[31]

The debts which Christ undertook to pay for the elect were the debts of obeying the law and the punishment owed to the elect by God for their transgression. Finally, since the covenant of grace had the character of a testament or will, the Second Person undertook to be the Testator by whose death the blessings of the testament and covenant would be bequeathed to the elect.

The Holy Spirit also gave His full consent to the scheme of salvation. This is seen in the fact that Christ was conceived in the Virgin Mary by the Holy Spirit and in that Christ offered His sacrifice to the Father through the Eternal Spirit (Hebrews 9. 14). Indeed, it was He who sealed all the promises of the covenant and has therefore been called the "Holy Spirit of promise" (Ephesians 1. 13). He also consented to work in the hearts of the elect and bring them, through regeneration and sanctification, to eternal glory.

At the basis of all the theological thinking of the three theologians whom we are studying there stood this conception of the eternal covenant of free grace, absolute and unconditional in its promises, and, as far as the elect are concerned, destined to be surely fulfilled in its historical manifestation. In the theological turmoil of their environment, and through their own inward trials, they found assurance and solace in this doctrine. It was for them a sure anchor on which their minds and hearts could rest.

Naturally they believed that this eternal covenant of grace was revealed in time in human history and in two basic forms of administration: the New Covenant, promised in the Old Testament and inaugurated by Christ, and the Mosaic Covenant, which was of a temporary nature. In the next chapter we shall discuss some of the blessings for the elect in the New Covenant.

THE COVENANT OF WORKS[32]

Like the majority of Puritans, the Hyper-Calvinists were Federal Theologians. Thus they held that God made a covenant of works with Adam, and, as we shall see in the next chapter, this covenant had an important place in their thought.

Since God, the Sovereign Ruler and Judge of all men, rules rational creatures by law, it was believed that God gave to His first creation, Adam, His law to obey as his part of the covenant of works. He engraved the moral law in his conscience and also revealed to him those regulations which governed his behaviour in the Garden of Eden. They described this covenant in various ways—"a covenant of friendship", "a legal covenant" and "a covenant of nature". It had two sacraments, paradise and the tree of life. However, since it was a contract God promised to bless and provide for Adam as long as he obeyed the divine law.

GOD, HIS DECREES AND COVENANTS

It is important to note that the Hyper-Calvinists believed that Adam did not act as a private individual in this covenant but as the federal and representative head of the whole human race. When he agreed to the terms of the covenant, he agreed on behalf of all people and when God promised life for complete obedience, He promised it to all people, and also when God threatened death for transgression, He meant it to refer both to Adam and to his posterity. Thus, when Adam did actually sin, he involved the whole human race in his guilt and his corruption. But he did not free his descendants from the obligation to obey the moral law of God as the only means of pleasing God and going to heaven.

Calvinism and Hyper-Calvinism

We shall conclude this chapter with a brief comparison of Calvin's doctrines of God, His decrees and covenants, with those of the Hyper-Calvinists. This comparison will show just how far the three authors whom we are studying have moved from authentic Calvinism.

First, we may notice that Calvin did not believe that human reason, working in the sphere of natural religion, could rise to the heights of the knowledge of God which Gill and Brine admitted. The view of these two theologians was very similar to that of Zwingli in reference to whose views Calvin wrote:

> I deny not, indeed, that in the writings of philosophers we meet occasionally with shrewd and apposite remarks on the nature of God, though they invariably savour somewhat of giddy imagination. . . . The Lord has bestowed upon them some slight perception of his Godhead, that they might not plead ignorance as an excuse for their impiety, and has, at times, instigated them to deliver some truths the confession of which should be their own condemnation. Still, though seeing, they saw not. Their discernment was not such as to direct them to the truth, far less to enable them to attain it, but resembled that of a bewildered traveller who sees the flash of lightning glance far and wide for a moment and then vanish into the darkness of the night, before he can advance a single step. . . . To the great truths, what God is in himself, and what he is in relation to us, human reason makes not the least approach.[33]

Secondly, Calvin was most careful not to apply logic too rigidly to Biblical doctrine. He certainly would have denied the principle advanced by Brine that logical deductions are to be made from Biblical premises. Indeed, he would have questioned whether in fact Biblical doctrines could be treated as premises at all!

Thirdly, Calvin held that the primary authority of Scripture rested in the work of the Holy Spirit making the words of Scripture become for the individual reader or hearer, the words of the living God. To a place of secondary importance Calvin relegated such proofs as the fulfilment of prophecy, miracles and other things. The Hyper-Calvinists put Calvin's secondary proofs to a place of primary importance. Also Calvin never enunciated the doctrine of the *literal* inspiration of Scripture although he held a very high view of its authority through the work of the Holy Spirit. "Though the letter (of Scripture)", wrote H. Clavier in reference to Calvin's view of Biblical inspiration, "does not escape from the control of the Spirit, it is for its content alone, for its spiritual content, that divine infallibility is claimed."[34]

Fourthly, and this we have noticed in Chapter I, Calvin believed that the doctrine of predestination can only be understood and appreciated when studied in reference to the work of Christ and the Holy Spirit. He deliberately refused to discuss this doctrine under the doctrine of God but placed it in the third book of the *Institutes* which deals with the application of redemption. Therefore we find no discussion of the eternal and immanent acts of God in Calvin's writings since he believed that our attention should be primarily focused on the Christ of history and not on the Christ of the decrees of God, or the Christ in the eternal thoughts of God. The writers to whom the Hyper-Calvinists turned for support for their description of the eternal and immanent acts of God were all very High Calvinists like Maccovius, Hoornbeck and Twisse.

Fifthly, as we also noticed in Chapter I, the growth of Federal Theology took place after the death of Calvin and therefore in his books there is to be found no discussion of the covenant of works[35] or of the covenant of grace as an eternal and immanent activity of God. His whole interest in the covenant of grace was in its manifestation in the history of

GOD, HIS DECREES AND COVENANTS 117

redemption.[36] The Hyper-Calvinists built their whole theological system around an advanced Federal Theology stressing the eternal nature of the covenant of grace and, as we shall see in the next chapter, deducing important conclusions from the covenant of works. In their references to previous writers there is no mention of Calvin but it is to such men as Witsius, Goodwin and Cocceius that they turn.

[1] Quoted by Stromberg, *op. cit.*, p. 1.
[2] Brine, *Treatise* . . ., pp. 69 ff. All references are to the 1813 edition.
[3] Gill, *Body of Divinity*, Vol. I, p. 34. All references are to the 1796 edition.
[4] Wayman, *Further Enquiry* . . . (1739), p. 85.
[5] Brine, *op. cit.*, p. 120.
[6] Brine, *Vindication of some truths* . . ., p. 55.
[7] Gill, *op. cit.*, pp. 19 ff.
[8] Gill, *Body of Divinity*, Vol. I, p. 45.
[9] Gill, *Doctrine of the Trinity* . . ., in *Sermons and Tracts*, Vol. III, p. 2.
[10] *Ibid*, pp. 12 ff.
[11] For original Sabellianism see Kelly, *Early Christian Doctrines*, pp. 121 ff.
[12] Gill, *Body of Divinity*, Vol. I, p. 205.
[13] *Ibid*, p. 207.
[14] *Ibid*, p. 210.
[15] *Ibid*, pp. 210 ff. For Brine's views see *Proper Eternity of the . . . Decrees*.
[16] Cf. Heppe, *Reformed Dogmatics*, pp. 133 ff.
[17] Gill, *op. cit.*, Vol. I, p. 252.
[18] Brine, *op. cit.*, pp. 8 ff.
[19] Gill, *Body of Divinity*, Vol. I, pp. 258 ff.
[20] In his frequent use of this phrase, Gill showed how much he had absorbed from the continental *scholastic* Calvinists.
[21] Gill, *op. cit.*, Vol. I, p. 270.
[22] Brine, *Motives to Love and Unity among Calvinists* (1753).
[23] Gill, *op. cit.*, Vol. I, p. 288.
[24] The doctrine of eternal union was a favourite doctrine of the doctrinal antinomians and is a theme to which the Hyper-Calvinists often turn. Cf. Gill, *The Doctrine of God's Everlasting Love to His Elect*, and Brine, *Christ, the Object of God's Eternal Delight* (1761).
[25] Cf. Gill, *Body of Divinity*, Vol. I, pp. 295 ff., and Brine, *Motives to Love and Unity*, pp. 35 ff.
[26] Cf. Gill, *The Doctrine of Justification*.
[27] Cf. Heppe, *op. cit.*, pp. 543 ff.
[28] Brine, *A Defence of the Doctrine of Eternal Justification* (1732), and Gill, *Body of Divinity*, Vol. I, pp. 302 ff.
[29] Cf. Gill, *op. cit.*, Vol. I, pp. 306 ff., and Brine, *The Covenant of Grace open'd* (1734).
[30] Gill, *op. cit.*, Vol. I, p. 311.
[31] *Ibid*, p. 350.
[32] *Ibid*, pp. 461 ff.

[33] *Institutes*, Book II, Chapter 2, Section 18.
[34] Clavier, *Etudes sur le calvinisme*, p. 27, cited by Wendel, *Calvin*, p. 159.
[35] *Institutes*, Book II, Chapters 1-2.
[36] *Ibid*, Book II, Chapters 7-13.

CHAPTER VII

MAN, HIS SIN AND HIS SALVATION

Synopsis: 1. Sin. 2. The Active and Passive Obedience of Christ. 3. Limited Atonement. 4. Satisfaction. 5. Justification and Adoption. 6. Regeneration, Conversion and Sanctification. 7. Assurance. 8. Calvin and Hyper-Calvinism. 9. The Free Offer of the Gospel. 10. The Theology of "The Modern Question".

In this chapter we are to examine the application of the blessings of the eternal covenant of grace to sinful, elect men through Jesus Christ, the Mediator, and the Holy Spirit, the Advocate within. We shall see that it was in this sphere of theology that the Hyper-Calvinists, partly through the absorption of the rationalism of their day, made their distinctive additions to High Calvinism.

SIN

The eighteenth century was certainly not an age in which the orthodox Reformed doctrine of the depravity of human nature was popular.[1] Accordingly, the Hyper-Calvinists felt obliged to insist upon this teaching both in the pulpit and in their books.[2]

They held that human nature was no longer pure and perfect as it had been in Adam before his fall. Not only was it deprived of the original principle of holiness and cut off from spiritual communion with God, but it was also under the constant dominion of sin as its governing principle. They believed that a human being had no spiritual understanding of the ways or things of God, and was each moment constantly offending the divine majesty.

The sinful state of each and every human being was traced back to the original sin of Adam who disobeyed God's will. Since Adam was considered as a representative head of all humanity, God reckoned his transgression and subsequent guilt as that of all his descendants, and thus the punishment due to him became due to them. Yet as the representative headship of Adam was related to his seminal relationship to the human race, the depraved nature of Adam was passed on to his descendants as well.

THE ACTIVE AND PASSIVE OBEDIENCE OF CHRIST

As we have already seen, Reformed theology taught that God had in eternity made plans for the fall of man, although He, Himself, took no part in human sin. In the eternal covenant of grace Christ agreed to become man and satisfy for the elect the requirements of God's holy, moral law, both in its demands for holy living and in its punishment of guilty offenders. Reformed theology called this twofold relationship to the law the active and passive obedience of Christ which were seen as two parts of His humiliation.[3] The Hyper-Calvinists adopted this distinction.[4]

Christ was "made of a woman, made under the law" (Galatians 4. 4). By birth, Jesus Christ was a Jew, subject to Jewish civil law. By being circumcised He became a religious Jew, subject to the ceremonial law. And being a human being He was subject to the moral law of the Creator. Also, He had to render obedience to His human parents as well as to the will of His heavenly Father. Though He did obey the civil, ceremonial, parental and divine will, His active obedience, which He rendered as the Surety of the elect, was to the moral law of the Creator. Christ obeyed in a perfect manner both the inner and outward requirements of this law. He loved God with all His heart, soul, mind and strength and loved His neighbour as He loved Himself.

Christ suffered in Gethsemane and died on the Cross of Calvary, not because He Himself deserved death, but because those whom He represented as Surety deserved to be punished and to die on account of their sins. His passive obedience consisted in His willingness to endure shame, suffering and even brief separation in His humanity from God. "He became obedient unto death, even the death of the Cross" for the sake of the elect and at the wish of the Father.

Thus the Hyper-Calvinists held that the elect were saved through both the active and passive righteousness of Christ.

Limited Atonement

Surrounded by many preachers who taught that Christ died for each and every man, Wayman, Gill and Brine were emphatic that Christ died only for the elect. This dogma frequently appears in their books and printed sermons. In answer to Isaac Watts' scheme of universal redemption,[5] Brine gave seven reasons why Christ could only have died for the elect.[6]

His first argument was based on the nature and the effects of God's love. Though God's love is necessarily infinite and eternal, its effects are only to be seen in a limited number of people. Only a few can say with the Apostle John: "Behold, what manner of love the Father hath bestowed upon us that we should be called the sons of God". The infinite love of God is obviously only directed at a certain number of people and these are they for whom Christ died. If He died for all, then all would be sons of God.

Secondly, he argued that since God has the praise and glory of His grace as well as the vindication of His justice in view in the whole drama of salvation, and since Christ has in view the personal satisfaction that He has redeemed sinners, Christ must have died for a specific number in order to be assured of attaining these ends. If He had died merely to gain a conditional salvation for all, the certainty of these ends would not have been assured.

Thirdly, he showed that Scripture describes the people for whom Christ died as "sheep" (John 10. 15), "sons" (Hebrews 2. 10), the "Church" (Ephesians 5. 25), the "body" (Ephesians 5. 23), and as "elect" (Romans 8. 23). Others are called "the rest" (Romans 11. 7), "the world" (John 17. 9), "goats" (Matthew 25. 33) and represented as "appointed unto condemnation" (Jude 4). The use of these different terms means that Christ died for only a part of the population of the world.

Fourthly, he showed that Scripture represents mankind as under one or two covenant heads, Adam and Christ. Not all the descendants of Adam are in the new humanity with Christ as its Head, and it was for this new humanity alone that Christ died, as the fifth chapter of Paul's letter to the Romans makes clear.

His fifth argument was taken from the description of the death of Christ as a redemption (*e.g.* I Peter 1. 18-19). The word usually has reference to the deliverance of criminals or slaves from deserved or imposed penalties. When a redemption price is paid, it is paid for a specific end and a certain number of criminals is set free. The death of Christ was obviously not a redemption price for the whole world since only a small part of the world's population is actually being redeemed. Thus He died and paid a redemption for the elect only.

His sixth argument was based on the fact that God is a just Judge. The Bible clearly declares that there will be a judgement at the end of the world when some people will be punished (Matthew 25). But the Bible also teaches that Christ bore the punishment of God to men (Galatians 3. 13). Yet God cannot punish people twice for the same sins and therefore Christ cannot have been made a curse for all men because if He had been there would be no need for a judgement and for punishments at the end of the world.

His seventh argument proceeded on the basis that Christ was a true High Priest. In His High Priestly prayer in John 17, Christ prayed not for the world but for those whom the Father had given Him out of the world. The Old Testament teaches that a priest only prays for those on whose behalf he offers sacrifice. This being so, Christ as Priest only offered Himself as a Sacrifice for the elect.

Gill gave similar arguments both in his *Body of Divinity* and in his defence of particular redemption in his *The Cause of God and Truth*. There is little doubt that the Hyper-Calvinists interpreted the atonement in the light of the decree of election and as a logical deduction from it. All their arguments for limited atonement proceeded on the basis that God had made such a decree.

Satisfaction

As the Socinian denial of the orthodox doctrine of Christ's vicarious death was widespread in the eighteenth century, the Hyper-Calvinists gave an important place in their thinking and writing to the doctrine of Christ's Satisfaction. Gill defined Satisfaction in these words:

> What Christ has done and suffered, in the room and stead of sinners, with content, with well pleasedness, and acceptance in the sight of God, is what may, with propriety, be called Satisfaction.[7]

It was constantly emphasised that Satisfaction was necessary since all the elect are sinners by nature. Sin is not merely a pecuniary debt which men owe to God; it is a criminal debt which God must punish. Men, as sinners, have not only broken the law but have incurred by their disobedience its curse and condemnation. God cannot merely, out of His good pleasure, forgive sin as if it were just a small debt of money. The moral law is an eternal expression of His holy nature and any breach of it is an offence to God Himself. Thus God must punish the offender; He can do no other. The Gospel states that Christ became the Surety of the elect and willingly received from the Judge of all men the punishment due to the elect. God satisfied His justice by punishing His Son. As Gill put it:

> What Christ bore, being laid upon him and imputed to him, were sins, all sorts of sins, original and actual; sins of every kind, open and secret, of heart, lip and life.[8]

By His sacrifical death Christ expiated these sins and offered the propitation to His Father. The result is as Brine wrote:

> God cannot but punish sin, either in the sinner or in a Surety for him; and since he has punished sin in Christ the Surety, he cannot but forgive, and omit to inflict punishment on the offender.[9]

Thus Satisfaction by Christ brought full and free forgiveness for the elect for sins past, present and future.

Justification and Adoption[10]

In the last chapter we saw that the Hyper-Calvinists regarded justification as an immanent and eternal act of God. They also held that the elect were virtually justified in the justification of their Surety, Christ, when He arose from the dead (Romans 4. 25). Eternal justification was pronounced in view of the (future) certainty of Christ gaining in His humanity a perfect righteousness, which was imputed to the elect.

It was held that the actual justification of each elect sinner during his earthly pilgrimage was caused by the work of the Holy Spirit in the heart. It is He alone, was the belief of Wayman, Gill and Brine, who convinces an elect sinner of His need of righteousness, Who grants the gift of saving faith to the enlightened elect sinner and Who finally pronounces the sentence of justification in his conscience, and declares to him that he is forgiven and accepted by God for Christ's sake.

Unlike the majority of Reformed divines,[11] they did not believe that God's attitude was changed towards a person when that person exercised saving faith in Christ. Each elect sinner realised at the time of his conversion that he was already justified in eternity and in the justification of his Surety. Indeed, for the Hyper-Calvinists, justification by faith meant a subjective realisation without any contemporaneous judicial declaration of acceptance by God, since this pronouncement had been made in eternity.

Adoption was also considered as an immanent and eternal act of God. The realisation and knowledge of eternal adoption is given to each elect soul at conversion, and there is no contemporaneous act of God accepting an elect sinner into His family.

REGENERATION, CONVERSION, SANCTIFICATION[12]

Since no unregenerate person is ready for or capable of enjoying the heavenly state and the holy fellowship which subsists between God and the saints in heaven, regeneration is necessary. This means:

the infusion of a new principle of spiritual life. . . . Men are dead in trespasses and sins, and therefore in order to their acting in a holy and a spiritual manner, a living, holy principle must be communicated to them.[13]

This new principle of life is produced in the elect by the infinite power and grace of God and is called in Scripture a "new nature" a "new spirit" and a "heart of flesh".

It was believed that regeneration is a work of God in which the elect person is wholly passive. It is an irresistible act of God's grace effected instantaneously in the soul by the Holy Spirit, and permanent in its nature. As a necessary result of this infusion of life warfare begins in the soul, the flesh lusting against the spirit, and the spirit against the flesh. Brine explained:

> The spiritual light which is communicated in regeneration enables a man to see the exceeding sinfulness of sin; he becomes now really acquainted with the malignity of sin, in its nature, as it is contrary to the law of God, which is a transcript of his infinitely pure and holy nature.[14]

The regenerate man also comes to see that "the wages of sin is death" and that he cannot contribute to his recovery out of this miserable condition; but the Holy Spirit creates within him a desire for salvation and a resolve to look for it in Christ, the Son of God. Thus he is led "to apply to Christ for pardon, peace, righteousness, grace, wisdom and strength".[15] Finally he turns from sin, self and Satan to God and is thereby converted through the gracious work of the Holy Spirit Who irresistibly makes him look to Christ.

Yet, as John Skepp had pointed out in *Divine Energy*, it was so easy to be deceived about the true nature of conversion. Brine devoted a whole chapter of his treatise to "the difference between real conversion and the semblance of it". First, he carefully distinguished between a legal conviction of sin and a spiritual conviction of sin. Legal conviction proceeds from a knowledge that one has broken the law of God and is guilty before the Judge of all men, but it does not include a true "godly sorrow" for sin. Spiritual conviction leads one to mourn because of one's sin, and to long for the gracious presence of God. Secondly, he believed that the knowledge of the Gospel which a "counterfeit" Christian has is so different from that enjoyed by the true Christian. The true Christian sees the glory and wisdom of God in the doctrines of the Gospel but the "counterfeit" Christian only knows that the doctrines are true because they come from God. Thirdly, the obedience given to God by the professing but not true Christian is of an entirely different nature from that offered to God by the true Christian. The former obeys God out of a sense of fear whilst the latter obeys God out of love and aims at His glory.

It was held that sanctification continues the work of God begun in the soul in the divine acts of regeneration and conversion. An essential part of sanctification is the fight against the principle of sin which remains in the heart of a regenerate man. This fight is mortification in which the old nature with all its sinful desires, is resisted, denied and not obeyed. The positive part of sanctification is vivification, which involves obeying God in the power of His grace. This is manifested in a holy reverence of God, a deep love for Him, a hearty submission to His will even in the most adverse dispensations of providence, a ready attendance at the means of grace, a desire for communion with God, and a love for His law and His truth.

Naturally the Hyper-Calvinists believed that those who are truly regenerate, effectually called, converted and being sanctified by the Spirit of God will persevere in grace to the end and be eternally saved. And they defended this belief against some who denied it.[16]

Assurance

We find in those sermons and tracts of the Hyper-Calvinists which deal with the reception of salvation by the individual, a great concern with the problem of how an individual may have the certain knowledge of election unto eternal life. The congregations who heard their sermons were called upon to examine themselves most carefully in order to ascertain whether or not they had inner proof of their election and whether their concern for the practice of religion was a merely legal attitude or a truly spiritual worship of God.

They were surrounded by many ministers and congregations that were unorthodox in doctrine but yet who (falsely) claimed the name of Christ. Thus, as we have already seen, they felt obliged to explain carefully, the true nature of conversion. Furthermore, their great emphasis upon the doctrines of election and the immanent acts of God made it imperative that much time and care be given to the act of deciding whether the signs in the hearts and lives were the genuine work of the Holy Spirit or not. Thus they continued the Puritan tradition of casuistry but because of the nature of the doctrines which they held, and the infidelity of the age in which they lived, they emphasised introspection and the examination of motives to a greater extent than many of their Puritan predecessors had done.

Brine believed that true assurance consisted of "a persuasion in the mind of a poor sinner of his particular interest in Christ and in His salvation".[17] This inner persuasion is partly, though not necessarily wholly, given to the believer at conversion.

> All believers have a proper and certain evidence within them of their interest in divine favour. Grace in the hearts of the saints is an effect of God's love to them, and his gracious purposes concerning them. And, therefore, from the being of grace in their souls, they may safely infer that they are objects of divine love, and interested in all those blessings which take rise therefrom.[18]

To maintain a calm assurance the individual believer must learn to distinguish between the motions of the flesh and those of the Spirit in order that he may not be submerged by doubts, fears and sin. He must also make full use of the means of grace and practise self-denial and watchfulness.

CALVIN AND HYPER-CALVINISM

At this point in our study we turn once more to a comparison of Calvinism with Hyper-Calvinism. In Chapter I we pointed out that John Calvin showed little, if any, interest in the doctrine of the imputation of Adam's sin to his descendants, because his primary concern was to expound the depravity of human nature, and to show how this had been inherited by the human race from the sinful nature acquired by Adam through his fall. Also Calvin, unlike Beza, did not divide the obedience of Christ into active and passive since his emphasis was upon the total obedience of Christ, the Suffering Servant, Who did the Father's will. Further, Calvin did not teach the specific doctrine of limited atonement. Thus in their doctrines of the imputation of Adam's sin, of the division of the righteousness of Christ into active and passive, and of limited atonement, the Hyper-Calvinists were following the High Calvinist tradition.

There are also wide differences in the two views of the reception of salvation by the individual Christian. Calvin only spoke of one form of justification and adoption, that which occurs at the moment of believing in Christ for salvation. He would have discounted eternal justification as an impious effort to pry into the mystery of God's purposes. For Calvin, union with Christ through living faith, and in the power of the Holy Spirit, was of supreme importance.[19] Thus union was not mystical but of a personal nature, bringing the believing sinner into a close, vital relationship with Christ, and God. Though the Hyper-Calvinists did not deny this dynamic relationship with Christ, they tended to concentrate upon obtaining a "saving interest" in Christ. They thought of their relation to Him as primarily covenantal, flowing from their "interest" through election in the eternal covenant of free grace. And this encouraged the idea that it was a legal relationship, an eternal right, and it pushed into the background the New Testament emphasis of a union of love between Saviour and saved.

It is because of this difference in the two views of the relationship of the believing sinner to the Saviour that Calvin's doctrine of assurance is much more Biblical and far less pragmatic than that of the Hyper-Calvinists. The true Calvinist doctrine of assurance of salvation knows nothing of the inner questionings and the introspection of the eighteenth-century "Calvinists". This is because its primary gaze is outward to Christ and not inward searching for signs of grace.[20]

We must now turn to the consideration of two doctrines taught by the Hyper-Calvinists, the teaching of which dis-

MAN, HIS SIN AND HIS SALVATION 129

tinguished them from those of their contemporaries who shared their zeal for the doctrines of High Calvinism. The first of these was the doctrine that they learned from Joseph Hussey that no purpose is served in offering the grace of Christ to all in the preaching of the Gospel. The second was the belief that it is not the duty of sinners who hear the Gospel to repent of their sins and believe on Christ for the forgiveness of sins.

The Free Offer of the Gospel

Unlike Hussey, neither Gill, Brine, nor Wayman produced a treatise specifically to defend the "no offers of grace" theology. Yet it was a belief that they all held and which determined the manner of their preaching and teaching, and to which they frequently allude in their books. We may illustrate this with a reference taken from three books, one of which was written by each of the three men.

John Gill had cause to refer to the doctrine in the book he wrote to defend the doctrine of absolute predestination against the criticisms of John Wesley. He wrote:

> The gospel is indeed ordered to be preached to every creature to whom it is sent and comes; but as yet, it has never been brought to all the individuals of human nature; there have been multitudes in all ages that have not heard it. And that there are universal offers of grace and salvation made to all men, I utterly deny; nay, I deny that they are made to any; no, not to God's elect; grace and salvation are provided for them in the everlasting covenant, procured for them by Christ, published and revealed in the gospel, and applied by the Spirit.[21]

Writing against the "Middle-Way" Calvinism of Isaac Watts, John Brine felt moved to write:

> But I am of opinion, that an Offer or Proposal for acceptance of New Covenant Blessings, is not made to Men, whilst they are under the old Covenant, or Law of Works, which are all men 'till regenerated, or so long as they are under the Dominion of Sin. *Offers* of grace as I conceive, are not made to those who are not under grace, nor interested in the Covenant of Grace, which many are not, to whom the Gospel is preached.[22]

In the midst of insisting that there are two types of people in the world, elect and reprobate, Wayman wrote:

And seeing . . . some have a right to life, pardon, communion with the Lord, yea, to the Son Himself, and others have not a right; is it comely for ministers of the Gospel of Christ to stand and offer grace, offer life and salvation to them that have no apparent right, nor yet a secret right?[23]

He went on to suggest that a minister should watch his congregation carefully and lead individuals to Christ as and when he saw the grace of God obviously working in them because it is not his business to offer grace to any but the regenerate.

The Hyper-Calvinists denied the free offer of the Gospel because they did not make a distinction between the eternal, secret will of God and the revealed will of God. (The former is known only to God, whilst the latter is revealed in the Bible.) They deduced the duty of the preacher from their knowledge of God's decrees rather than from His commands and invitations in Scripture. Calvin and the majority of Reformed divines had refused to take this logical, yet unscriptural, step. Commenting upon Hosea 13. 14, Calvin wrote:

> God does not here simply promise salvation, but shews that he is indeed ready to save, but that the wickedness of the people was an impediment in the way. "I will redeem them", as far as this depends on me. What, then, does stand in the way? Even the hardness of the people; for they would have preferred to perish a hundred times rather than turn to the Lord. . . . We may learn from this passage, that when men perish, God still continues like himself, and that neither his power, by which he is mighty to save the world, is extinguished, not his purpose changed, so as not to be always ready to help; but that the obstinacy of man rejects the grace which has been provided, and which God willingly and bountifully offers. . . .[24]

Expounding Hebrews 3. 3, John Owen wrote:

> They who are judged at the last day (for not receiving the Gospel) will be speechless and have nothing to reply. . . . Because *they despise an overture of a treaty about peace and reconciliation* between God and their souls. God who hath no need of them, nor their obedience or friendship, tenders them a treaty upon terms of peace. What greater condescension, love or grace could be conceived or desired? This is tendered in the Gospel, 2 Cor. 5. 19. Now what greater indignity can be offered unto him than to reject his tenders? Is not this plainly to tell him that they despise his love and scorn his offers of reconciliation? It is life and salvation that he tenders, on whose neglect he complains that men will not come unto him that they might have life. Certainly there can be no want of righteousness in the ruin of such persons.[25]

Many quotations could be added to these but they are sufficient to illustrate that the Hyper-Calvinist doctrine was an innovation and a serious departure from Reformed orthodoxy.

The Theology of "The Modern Question"

In the 1730s a controversy arose in Northamptonshire concerning the nature of faith and repentance required of sinners. It involved Matthias Maurice, successor of Richard Davis at Rothwell, and Lewis Wayman, of Kimbolton. Later it spread to London, where Thomas Bradbury, minister of the Congregational Church in Fetter Lane, Abraham Taylor, tutor and minister at Deptford, John Brine and John Gill took part. It also spread to the North of England involving Alverey Jackson, Baptist minister at Barnoldswick.[26]

Alverey Jackson stated what was the Modern Question in the title of his contribution to the controversy. His tract was, *The Question Answered. Whether saving faith in Christ is a duty required by the moral law of all those who live under the Gospel revelation* (1752). Matthias Maurice, Thomas Bradbury, Abraham Taylor and Alverey Jackson answered this question in the affirmative. They believed that the law of God, which demands of every man love and worship to God, necessarily commands all people to believe, with all their hearts, any revelation which God gives and any truth He publishes. As the Gospel contains the supreme revelation of God, all men are, through their solemn duty to worship God, obliged, not merely to give a mere general intellectual assent to it, but to believe it with their hearts, souls, minds and strength. This means that they will repent of their sins and accept God's grace which is offered to man in the good news. They argued that if God condemns men for not believing the Gospel, He must require them to believe it when they hear it. And since forgiveness is promised in the New Testament to the faith which the Gospel demands, then the faith which God requires is saving faith, not a general, vague kind of belief. In asserting this belief and doctrine these men were echoing the views of the majority of Reformed divines.

Wayman, Brine and Gill answered the question in the

negative. As they had already accepted the "no offers of grace" scheme, they were obliged, by a simple process of logical deduction, to assert that all men are not required to exercise saving faith in Christ when they hear the preaching of the Gospel. This assertion placed them in another theological problem because they also believed that the moral law is binding on all people in its demand for love to God and man. They faced this problem by insisting on the careful distinction between legal repentance and evangelical repentance and between common faith and saving faith. They held that the moral law only required a forsaking of sin and an attempt to live by its rule, along with an intellectual assent to all that God has said and revealed. Evangelical repentance and saving faith are not required by the moral law because they are gifts of the covenant of free grace, wrought in man by the irresistible grace of God. To prove their point they resorted to a discussion of what kind of faith God required of Adam in the covenant of works before his fall.

It was Lewis Wayman who first made use of this argument from Adam's relation to God;[27] but, as John Brine gave a rather more developed version of it in 1743, we shall give in full Brine's reasoning.

I

I apprehend, that whatever was, or could have been the Duty of Man upon the Supposition of a Revelation, super-added to what he enjoyed in his mere Creation-State, is the Duty of Men in their fallen state, upon the said Supposition.

II

That Man in his perfect State was bound to love, reverence and adore God: and that Men in their lapsed State are obliged to these Acts, notwithstanding their present Want of ability, in Consequence of the Fall.

III

That it was the Duty of Man in his primitive State, to believe the Truth and Importance of every Revelation he should receive from God; and that it is the Duty of Men in their fallen State so to do.

IV

But with Respect to special Faith in Christ, it seems to me, that the Powers of Man in his perfect State were not fitted and disposed to that Act. My reasons for this Thought are these:

1. The Communication of such a Power to Man, in his primitive State, would have been in vain; for there was no Necessity nor Use of believing in Christ in that State; and I humbly conceive that Man was not furnished with a Power, the Exertion of which was unnecessary, so long as he should remain in his perfect State.
2. Because God could not require Man, while in a perfect State, to put forth such an Act, as special Faith in Christ is. The reason is evident; this Act necessarily supposed a Dependence on Christ for Salvation, as Creatures lost and miserable in ourselves; but 'till Man was fallen and become miserable, he could not exercise such a Trust in Christ, as a Redeemer. And therefore, if it is supposed that God furnished Man, in a State of Innocence, with a Power of acting this special Faith in a Mediator, it must, I think, be allowed that he gave Man an Ability, which so long as he continued to possess it, he could not require him to exert.
3. Special faith in Christ belongs to the new Creation, of which he as Mediator between God and his People, is the Author; and therefore, I apprehend, that a Power of acting this special faith in him, was not given to Man by, or according to, the Law of his first Creation.
4. It seems to me a very extraordinary Dispensation, that Man should be furnished with a Power he could not exercise in his perfect State; and in his corrupt State be deprived of that Power, wherein alone the Exertion and Exercise of it can be necessary or useful.[28]

After the above reasons, Brine made the remarkable admission that he had found very similar arguments concerning the capacities of Adam in the *Apology* of Arminius, and that the scholastic Calvinist, Maccovius, had sought to refute the views of Arminius on this point.[29] This was a most remarkable admission by Brine since it was to the books of Maccovius that he turned for supporting testimony for his doctrines of eternal union and eternal justification, and since Arminianism was the theological system to which the Hyper-Calvinists showed the greatest animosity.

The Hyper-Calvinists made use of the distinction between legal and evangelical repentance, common and saving faith, in their exegesis of those passages in the Gospels and the Acts of the Apostles where Jesus or an Apostle calls upon the hearers to repent and believe. They held that God only required legal repentance and common faith of the majority of people in the crowds but did require evangelical repentance and saving faith of the regenerate, elect people who heard. In his explanation of the command of God to repent in the Acts of the Apostles 17. 30, Wayman stated that God only required legal repentance and then said:

> I am persuaded, it will one day appear to be a truth that God will have the outward report of the Gospel received, and the Bible received and kept by those, who have no special interest in the promise, and grace contain'd in it: that it may be in readiness for his hidden ones, where, and when it shall please him to give them grace, and call them out of darkness into his marvellous light in their appointed months.[30]

They put forward very few passages of Scripture to prove their opinions since they simply applied their hypothesis to all passages that were mentioned and to their own satisfaction they believed that their way of seeing things was the correct one.

After he had given his arguments concerning the capacities of Adam before the fall, Wayman proceeded to supply quotations from the writings of John Owen and Thomas Goodwin in order to show that they had held similar views to his own. (In his pamphlets, Brine did not make use of this appeal to the Puritans.) After showing that Owen believed that men need spiritual illumination to comprehend the mystery of the Gospel,[31] he gave three short quotations from Goodwin's *Of the Creatures*, after which he wrote:

> What can be plainer than that this is the Doctor's judgement? That Adam's knowledge is inferior to that which believers have by Christ; that he could not have gone to heaven, had he not fallen, without supernatural grace wrought in him; and that wicked men, now under the Gospel, are blamed only for not believing so far as such natural light, as was in him, would have enabled them to believe. It is evidently his judgement that we did not lose that faith, which is in the question, in *Adam*, because we had it not in him; and it is equally evident that his judgement was, that men are not condemned for not believing in Christ, because saith he, they are not blam'd for it; which is all I am contending for.[32]

In view of this appeal by Wayman to the two great Independent divines, we must briefly examine the thought of each one to see whether or not they did answer the Modern Question (before it was raised) in the negative.

First, let us look at the views of John Owen. As will be seen in the following quotation, there is little doubt that Owen believed that the minister of Christ should offer the grace of God freely to all hearers of the Gospel.

> We must exactly distinguish between man's duty and God's purpose, there being no connection between them. The purpose and decree of God is not the rule of our duty; neither is the performance of our duty in doing what we are commanded, any declaration of what is God's purpose to do, or his decree that it should be done. Especially is this to be seen and considered in the duty of the ministers of the gospel, in the dispensing of the word, in exhortations, invitations, precepts, and threatenings committed unto them; all which are perpetual declaratives of our duty, and do manifest approbation of the thing exhorted and invited to, with the truth of the connection between one thing and another, but not of the counsel and purpose of God, in respect of individual persons, in the ministry of the word. A minister is not to make enquiry after, nor to trouble himself about, those secrets of the eternal mind of God—namely, whom he purposeth to save, and whom he hath sent Christ to die for in particular. It is enough for them to search his revealed will, and thence take their *directions*, from whence they have their *commissions*. . . . They command and invite all to repent and believe; but they know not in particular on whom God will bestow repentance unto salvation, nor in whom he will effect the work of faith with power.[33]

The question now arises as to what kind of faith Owen believed that God required from those who heard the Gospel. He answered this with four propositions. It was the duty of unregenerate sinners to believe:

1. The truth of the Gospel in general.

2. That faith in Christ is the only way to salvation.

3. That every sinner stands in great need of a Saviour.

4. That there is a sufficiency in Christ which is able to save the sinner if that sinner gives himself up to Christ, in Christ's appointed way.[34]

These propositions contained, in Owen's view, the *necessary* beginnings of saving faith. What Owen did deny was the belief that the preacher should command his hearers to believe that Christ died for each and every one of them in particular. The possession of an inner conviction that Christ died for anyone is a gift of God to the regenerate.

Thus there seems to be little doubt that Owen did believe that the duty of hearers of the Gospel was to put forth saving faith in Christ even if the possession of saving faith is a gift of God. Though he was a firm believer in the doctrines of election and particular redemption, he nevertheless believed in the free offer of the Gospel to all and the duty of all to respond to that which the Gospel required, saving faith in Christ. There is no use made in his writings of the appeal to the powers of Adam to show the duty of men who live under the Gospel revelation. And if he did say that Adam would have needed spiritual illumination to comprehend the mystery of Christ, that was because he had such a high opinion of the Son of God, and of the superiority of the Gospel to even the highest form of natural religion.

The basic purpose of Goodwin's treatise, *Of the Creatures* is, through a contrast of Adam's original state with that of a man "in Christ", to show the superiority of the knowledge of God enjoyed by the Christian to that enjoyed by the perfect first man. Goodwin believed that Adam's knowledge of God was a *natural* knowledge only and thus his faith was merely a natural faith, whilst the knowledge of God enjoyed by a Christian is a supernatural knowledge.

> Adam's covenant was *foedus naturae*, so his happiness should have been a perfect contentment in God, enjoyed *per modum naturae*; not in God himself immediately, neither should he have tasted this heavenly contentment by faith, which is a prelibation of heaven and of its beatifical vision, but only in effects. The creatures should have revealed God unto him, and been as testimonies of his favour, which he should have apprehended as justifying and approving him in a covenant of works; which apprehension would have brought peace of conscience, joy and security therein through well-doing, so far as the persuasion of God's love, which conscience and his own spirit begat in him, which was his comforter, could work.[35]

Yet this belief that Adam's faith was purely a natural faith (with its corollary that Adam's future life only had reference to immortality in the Garden and not in heaven) was not the general Reformed view, a fact which Goodwin readily admitted.

> As the conclusion of this discourse, because I would not maintain a dispute against a multitude of divines who are of another mind in their writings, if we will grant and suppose that there was such a light of faith

vouchsafed to Adam as was superior to the law of nature specified (whereby he knew God in his works and such revelations as externally carried their own evidence with them), even unto natural faith, and to have been as supernatural as ours, yet still the assertion I aim at will hold true, that a believer's knowing of God, and enjoying of him, doth infinitely transcend that of his in many respects.[36]

Thus, in turning to Goodwin for support Wayman was on firm ground if he wanted support for his belief that Adam's faith was only a natural faith. We must now look at the one passage in the treatise in which Goodwin wrote something relevant to the Modern Question.

Wicked men are blamed now for not believing the word of the law and gospel so far as such natural light as was in Adam would have enabled them thereunto seeing the law given was confirmed at first by such works and voices, as evidently would have argued to that first natural light that it was God that spake it, and they, if they had that light remaining, would have owned in their hearts. And the gospel also delivered by Christ was confirmed by signs and wonders: Hebrews ii. 3, 4, "How shall we escape if we neglect so great salvation; which at the first began to be spoken by the Lord, and was confirmed unto us by them that heard him; God also bearing them witness, both with signs and wonders, and with diverse miracles, and gifts of the Holy Ghost, according to his own will?" And the whole word written, derived to us, and then delivered, hath such peculiar characters of divine authority engraven upon it, so as even to natural light (if we had it pure as Adam had) would evidence itself to be of God, and so bind all men to believe it. And therefore men are both justly commanded to believe it, and justly blamed for not believing it.[37]

Thus it seems that Wayman was right to believe that Goodwin taught that men are only to accept the Gospel with natural faith. Goodwin's desire to exalt the heavenly life in Christ led him to minimise the life in God enjoyed by the perfect Adam. Yet we must add that, as far as is known, Goodwin never questioned the right of the preacher to offer the grace of the Gospel to all who hear the Word preached. Furthermore, his printed sermons which deal with the subject of repentance certainly give the impression that he called the unregenerate to more than a legal repentance and a natural faith.[38]

As we noticed in Chapter III, Thomas Goodwin, who took part in the Antinomian controversy, had no doubt at all that the law of God, speaking through the Gospel, commanded men to repent and to believe with saving faith on the Lord Jesus Christ. Indeed, Thomas Goodwin Jnr., Matthias Maurice, Thomas Bradbury, Abraham Taylor, Alverey Jackson, and the majority of Reformed divines were all of one mind on this question; they believed that the law, speaking through the Gospel, required all hearers of the Gospel to accept its offered grace.

[1] Cf. Colligan, *Arian Movement in England*, pp. 97-98. One of the most devastating criticisms of the orthodox view was written by John Taylor of Norwich, *The Scripture-Doctrine of Original Sin* (1738).
[2] Cf. Gill, *Body of Divinity*, Vol. I, pp. 468 ff., and the relevant parts of *Cause of God and Truth*. Cf. also Brine, *Treatise*, pp. 38 ff.
[3] Cf. Heppe, *op. cit.*, pp. 448 ff.
[4] Cf. Gill, *Body of Divinity*, Vol. II, pp. 75 ff., and Brine, *The Imputation of Christ's Active Obedience to His people* (1759).
[5] Watts, *The Ruin and Recovery of Mankind* (1740).
[6] Brine, *The Certain Efficacy of the Death of Christ* (1743), pp. 4 ff. He actually gives eight reasons but we have joined the sixth and seventh.
[7] Gill, *op. cit.*, Vol. II, p. 191. It is interesting to note that in their doctrine of Satisfaction, Gill and Brine do not follow Goodwin, Twisse and Rutherford. Gill and Brine derived the necessity of Satisfaction from the nature of God, His offended justice and righteousness. Goodwin, Twisse and Rutherford derived the necessity of Satisfaction from the divine will. God could, they argued, forgive sin without Satisfaction if He so pleased.
[8] *Ibid*, p. 203.
[9] Brine, *op. cit.*, p. 203.
[10] Cf. Gill, *Body of Divinity*, Vol. II, pp. 228 ff., and Brine, *Vindication of some truths . . .*, Chapter xi.
[11] Cf. A. A. Hodge, *The Confession of Faith*, pp. 179 ff.
[12] Cf. Gill, *Body of Divinity*, Vol. II, pp. 268 ff., and Brine, *Treatise*, pp. 126 ff.
[13] Brine, *op. cit.*, p. 131.
[14] *Ibid*, p. 134.
[15] *Ibid*, p. 137.
[16] *E.g.* Gill, *The Doctrine of the Saints' Final Perseverance*, which was written against the Wesleyan doctrine that a Christian could fall permanently from grace.
[17] Brine, *Treatise*, p. 156.
[18] *Ibid*, pp. 151-2.
[19] Cf. Wendel, *Calvin*, pp. 233 ff.
[20] Cf. Wallace, *Calvin's Doctrine of the Christian Life*.
[21] Gill, *Doctrine of Predestination . . .*, in *Sermons and Tracts*, Vol. III, p. 271.
[22] Brine, *Certain Efficacy . . .*, p. 75.
[23] Wayman, *Further Enquiry . . .*, p. 50.
[24] Calvin, *Hosea* (*C.T.S.E.*), (1857), pp. 476-7.
[25] Owen, *Works* (ed. Goold), Vol. XX, p. 308.

MAN, HIS SIN AND HIS SALVATION

[26] For the history of the controversy see G. F. Nuttall, "Northampton and 'The Modern Question', a turning-point in eighteenth-century Dissent", *J. Th. S.*, N.S. XVI, Part I, 1965. For Barnoldswick see Whitley, *Baptists of North-West England*, pp. 83 ff.

[27] Wayman, *Further Enquiry after Truth*, pp. 51 ff.

[28] Brine, *Refutation of Arminian Principles*, pp. 4 ff.

[29] An English translation of the *Apology* is to be found in the *Writings of James Arminius*, Vol. I, pp. 276 ff. Arminius expressed his view as follows: "I profess and teach that before his fall, Adam had not the power to believe in Christ because faith in Christ was not then necessary; and that God therefore could not require this faith from him after the fall", p. 332. The views of Maccovius are in *Loci Communes*, Chap. 44.

[30] Wayman, *op. cit.*, p. 128.

[31] Wayman's brief quotation is from Owen's *The Causes, Ways and Means of Understanding the Mind of God as revealed in His Word* (1678) which is part of his famous *Discourse on the Holy Spirit*. In the passage quoted, Owen is arguing that even intelligent men need the illumination of the Holy Spirit to understand the spiritual truths of the Bible. It is not Owen's purpose to discuss the capacities of Adam before the fall in relation to the Gospel which was proclaimed after the fall. Wayman, therefore, quoted out of context, and even changed (or wrongly transcribed) various words.

[32] *Ibid*, p. 58.

[33] Owen, *The Death of Death in the Death of Christ* (new edition 1959), pp. 187-8.

[34] *Ibid*, p. 296.

[35] Goodwin, *Of the Creatures and the condition of their state by creation*, in *Works*, Vol. VII, p. 53.

[36] *Ibid*, p. 67.

[37] *Ibid*, p. 56.

[38] Cf. Goodwin, *On Repentance*, in *Works*, Vol. VII, pp. 543 ff.

PART FOUR
CONCLUSION

CHAPTER VIII

A DEFINITION OF HYPER-CALVINISM

Synopsis: 1. Terminology. 2. Definition of Hyper-Calvinism. 3. The Factors involved in the change from High to Hyper-Calvinism. 4. The Continuance and Effects of Hyper-Calvinism. 5. Andrew Fuller and Evangelical Calvinism.

In this study we have reserved the term "Calvinism" for the theology of John Calvin. We have used the term "High Calvinism" to describe the result of the hardening of Calvinism by Beza and many Reformed theologians after him. From about the year 1600 High Calvinism was, in many cases combined with, or even tempered by, Federal Theology. The great Puritan document, the Westminster Confession of Faith, combined both High Calvinism and Federal Theology, and the same fusion of dogma is found in the writings of such leading Puritans as William Ames and John Owen. Of course there were degrees of High Calvinism amongst the Puritans as well as the presence of Moderated Calvinism. Some theologians (*e.g.* Perkins and Twisse) were supralapsarians but the majority of Puritans were infralapsarians. A few divines (*e.g.* Twisse and Pemble) taught the doctrine of eternal justification although the greater number preferred to speak only of justification by faith and perhaps virtual justification in the resurrection of Christ. Yet all High Calvinists of the seventeenth century regarded the "Five Points of Calvinism" formulated at the Synod of Dort as containing the essence of Protestant thought. These were: first the total depravity of man and his inability to save himself; secondly, unconditional personal election; thirdly, particular redemption; fourthly, the efficacious call of the Spirit, and finally, the final perseverance of the saints. To these many added a Federal Theology, a view that the Bible is inerrant, and an emphasis on assurance of salvation. Also, with very few exceptions, Reformed divines in England and on the continent carefully distinguished between the secret and the revealed will of God and refused to deduce the duty of minister and people from anything but the revealed will of God.

The terms "False Calvinism" and "High Calvinism" were used in the latter part of the eighteenth century to describe what we have described as "Hyper-Calvinism". It was only in the nineteenth century that the expression Hyper-Calvinism came to be generally used to describe the same doctrinal system which some people in the eighteenth century called High Calvinism. Yet men like Andrew Fuller, who made use of the latter term (as well as "False" and "Hyper-Calvinism") did not make any deliberate distinction between the theology of Calvin and that found in the Westminster Confession of Faith. Thus they did not feel the need of a term to distinguish the "Calvinism" of the Puritans from that of Calvin. But since there is a difference between Calvin's theology and that of men like William Ames and John Owen, and between these orthodox Puritans and men like John Gill and John Brine, there is need for three terms. We have used "Calvinism", "High Calvinism" and "Hyper-Calvinism".

It would be preferable to use a term to describe the theology of Hussey, Skepp, Wayman, Gill and Brine which did not make use of Calvin's name, but since these men did use the term "Calvinism" to describe their own theology, to avoid a term that dispensed with his name would not be practicable.

DEFINITION OF HYPER-CALVINISM

Perhaps at this point we should seek to supply a definition of Hyper-Calvinism. It was a system of theology, or a system of the doctrines of God, man and grace, which was framed to exalt the honour and glory of God and did so at the expense of minimising the moral and spiritual responsibility of sinners to God. It placed excessive emphasis on the immanent acts of God—eternal justification, eternal adoption and the eternal covenant of grace. In practice, this meant that "Christ and Him crucified", the central message of the apostles, was obscured. It also often made no distinction between the

A DEFINITION OF HYPER-CALVINISM 145

secret and the revealed will of God, and tried to deduce the duty of men from what it taught concerning the secret, eternal decrees of God. Excessive emphasis was also placed on the doctrine of irresistible grace with the tendency to state that an elect man is not only passive in regeneration but also in conversion as well. The absorbing interest in the eternal, immanent acts of God and in irresistible grace led to the notion that grace must only be offered to those for whom it was intended. Finally, a valid assurance of salvation was seen as consisting in an inner feeling and conviction of being eternally elected by God. So Hyper-Calvinism led its adherents to hold that evangelism was not necessary and to place much emphasis on introspection in order to discover whether or not one was elect.

Yet it did not lead, at least in the lives of the men whom we have studied, to practical antinomianism, although they were called antinomians by many of their contemporaries.[1] Skepp, Hussey, Wayman, Gill and Brine were noted for their austere, exemplary characters and they all believed that the life of an elect believer should be ruled inwardly and outwardly by the moral law of God.

A brief comparison of some of the emphases of Hyper-Calvinism with the doctrines advocated by the Lime Street lecturers in 1731-2 will show that the use of "Hyper-Calvinism" is justified. In his lecture on justification, Robert Bragge carefully showed that the Bible teaches that a sinner is not justified until he believes on Christ.[2] In 1732 John Brine published a *Defence of the doctrine of eternal justification*. Both John Hurrion and Samuel Wilson carefully distinguished the secret and the revealed will of God in regard to the duty of sinners who hear the Gospel.[3] The Hyper-Calvinists did not make this distinction. Abraham Taylor made reference to "some ignorant enthusiastick preachers" who insisted much "on eternal union with Christ, and that sin could do no harm to a believer".[4] He had in mind the doctrinal antinomianism of such men as John Saltmarsh, John Eaton and Tobias Crisp, whose views were opposed by the Westminster Assembly in 1643. Replying to this charge by Taylor, John Gill defended the doctrines of Saltmarsh, Crisp and Eaton in his *Doctrines of God's Everlasting Love to His Elect*, and in 1755 edited a new edition of Crisp's sermons.

The Factors Involved in the Change from High to Hyper-Calvinism

The forces which were at work in the latter part of the seventeenth and the first part of the eighteenth centuries to cause the development of High Calvinism into Hyper-Calvinism were many and varied. To document them all, or even to ascertain what they all were, is impossible. All that we can do is to suggest four factors each of which played an important part in causing this transition.

First, we may note that after the Restoration in 1660 orthodox Calvinism became, as it were, a cause under siege. The majority of Puritans who were orthodox Calvinists left the Church of England in 1662 to become Nonconformists. Thus the religious leadership of the nation was lodged firmly in the hands of men who were either Arminian or moderately Calvinistic in theology. The ejected ministers, being Nonconformists, were placed under harsh and cruel restrictions until 1688 and this severely curtailed their influence upon the religious thought of the nation. As the older men died their places were taken by younger men who had been educated under liberalising influences in Holland and so a Moderated Calvinism gradually became popular, especially amongst the Presbyterian Dissenters. As the years passed by High Calvinism became more and more the sole preserve of the Independents and the Particular Baptists. The Antinomian controversy of the 1690s served to widen the gap between High Calvinism and Moderated Calvinism, and as the eighteenth century passed by, High Calvinism became in the main, the faith of the poorly-educated Independents and Baptists.[5] These men who clung to the doctrines of High Calvinism saw themselves as a group preserved by God in an apostate age to defend "the faith once delivered to the saints". Their time was taken up by the defence of their faith and it was in this atmosphere of a cause under siege that Hyper-Calvinism was born and nurtured.

Secondly, between 1689 and 1765, High Calvinism was placed in an environment which emphasised the role of reason in religious faith. This meant that the High Calvinists were in danger either of absorbing the rationalism, or of rejecting it completely, or of doing both. It would seem that Joseph Hussey fell prey to both temptations. He absorbed the rationalistic tendencies of his day and applied strict logic to Biblical doctrines so that from the doctrines of eternal election and irresistible grace he deduced that Christ should not be offered to all men. And also he deduced from the part which he believed that Christ played in the covenant of grace the doctrine that Christ's humanity was "standing in God" before the creation of the world. One of Hussey's followers, Samuel Stockell, abandoned the doctrine of eternal generation because he could not conceive how "the Begetter and the Begotten" could be of equal date. Wayman, Gill and Brine applied logic to the (hypothetical) covenant of works and deduced the doctrine that it is not the duty of hearers of the Gospel to believe on the Lord Jesus Christ. Yet all these men believed that they were not being rationalistic in a human sense but were simply applying "evangelical reason", or reason inspired by the Holy Spirit, to the Bible's teaching.

Thirdly, the personal backgrounds of the Hyper-Calvinists must also be taken into consideration. Joseph Hussey seems to have been a man who was capable of making extreme changes in his thought. Ordained by Presbyterian ministers in 1688, he became, after 1693, a Congregationalist. In 1693 he published a book which strongly advocated the free offer of Christ to men in preaching; but, in 1707, he published another book which advocated just as strongly the opposite notion. In 1691 he opposed Richard Davis whilst in 1706 he was happy to have his theology called "Davisism". The other men whom we studied were all self-educated. They were brought up in a closed environment and never had the chance to pursue theological studies in a Scottish or Dutch University or an English Academy. They had chosen their brand of theology before they had examined any others. Had Hussey been of a more stable disposition, and the other men educated in the environment of a Reformed University or Academy, the story of Hyper-Calvinism might have been very different.

Fourthly, the Hyper-Calvinists were sincere men of average intelligence, but they lacked a prophetical and discerning spirit. They keenly desired to glorify God and mistakenly believed that God was more glorified by the exaltation of free grace in the pulpit and on the printed page, than in the evangelism and conversion of men. They became so obsessed with the defence of what they regarded as sound doctrine that the evangelistic note of Scripture as basically an overture by God towards sinners was muted. This lack of interest in evangelism (and a reference to evangelism in their books is virtually impossible to find) came, as we have seen, with the deduction of the duty of ministers in preaching from the secret will of the Lord, the will of His decrees. They did not realise what a baneful influence their doctrines would have upon those who followed in their footsteps.

The Continuance and Effects of Hyper-Calvinism

Throughout the eighteenth and nineteenth centuries, there were people who continued to find Hyper-Calvinism attractive and who reprinted the writings of Hussey, Skepp, Bentley, Wayman, Gill and Brine as well as writing more books on the same lines. Hussey's *Glory of Christ* was, in various editions, reprinted in 1761, 1790, 1822, 1836, 1844 and 1846, and his *God's Operations of Grace* had its third edition in 1792 and its fourth in 1851. Bentley's *The Lord the Helper of His People* was reprinted in 1848 and contained, as in the first edition, the last dying words of Joseph Hussey. Skepp's *Divine Energy* had a second edition in 1751 and a third in 1815. Brine's *Treatise* was in its fourth edition by 1813 and its fifth in 1853. Wayman's *Further Enquiry* was reprinted in 1802. Many of John Gill's sermons and tracts were reprinted in three large volumes after his death in 1773. His *Body of Divinity* and his *Exposition of the Old and New Testaments* went through at least four editions, whilst his *Cause of God and Truth* was reprinted as recently as 1962 in the U.S.A.

Another person who assisted in the progagation of Hyper-Calvinism was Mrs. Ann Dutton, to whom we have already made a brief reference. As Ann Williams she was brought up in Northampton and eventually attached herself to the church over which John Moore was the pastor. She married a man named Mr. Coles and, when living with him in London, regularly heard John Skepp preach. After the death of Mr. Coles she married Benjamin Dutton, with whom in 1732 she went to live in Great Gransden, a village in Huntingdonshire, where Dutton became pastor of the small Baptist church. From here Ann Dutton scattered her tracts, books, poems and letters. Her chief literary production, which went through at least six editions and which reflected the supralapsarian Hyper-Calvinism of Hussey and Skepp was entitled, *A Narration of the Wonders of Grace in Verse: to which is added a poem on the special work of the Spirit in the hearts of the Elect*. In the middle of the nineteenth century, J. A. Jones, the author of *Bunhill Memorials*, spoke of her as the "celebrated" Ann Dutton. She died in 1765.

Yet another person, to whom we have only made brief reference, who helped to spread the doctrine of Hyper-Calvinism was Samuel Stockell. His views on the God-Man gained acceptance amongst many Particular Baptists so that John Brine in 1754, and Andrew Fuller thirty years later, had to make reference to them. John Macgowan (1726-1780), minister of Devonshire Square Particular Baptist Church from 1767 to 1780, likewise taught that the human soul of Christ was joined to His divine nature in heaven before the creation of the world and so also did John Allen, a Baptist minister, and author of *Royal Spiritual Magazine* (1752). In the first part of the nineteenth century, Stockell's views were adopted by John Stevens (1776-1847), another Particular Baptist minister. Stevens also shared the views of Wayman, Gill and Brine in regard to the duty of sinners and opposed Andrew Fuller on this point. But through the writings of Stevens on the question of Christology, there was a serious controversy about the doctrine of eternal generation amongst Strict and Particular Baptists in the 1830s and 1840s which resulted in the formation of a group of Baptists who are now called the Gospel Standard Strict Baptists.[6]

The combined influence of the Hyper-Calvinists mentioned above was to produce in the Churches connected with them, and amongst those whom they influenced, a tendency only to maintain their Churches but not to expand them. Of John Gill's particular influence, C. H. Spurgeon wrote: "The system of theology with which many identify his name has chilled many Churches to their very soul, for it has led them to omit the free invitations of the Gospel".[7] Also, as W. T. Whitley has pointed out, in the very years when Gill shut himself in his study to expound the New Testament, George Whitefield was preaching several times daily to thousands of people on Newington Common, Blackheath, and Kennington Common; and in the same year that Brine published a refutation of the tract, *The Modern Question*, Newton of Olney went to Moorfields and by the light of lanterns saw Whitefield preaching to thousands, leading to repentance on one occasion more than eleven times as many sinners as there were saints listening to Brine a quarter of a mile away.[8] The spirit which Hyper-Calvinism bred is seen in old John C. Ryland's shout from the chair when William Carey suggested the formation of a missionary society: "Sit down, young man; when God pleases to convert the heathen He will do it without your aid or mine". It is a fact that to this day the Gospel Standard Strict Baptist Churches officially support no missionary societies. However, the more liberal Strict Baptists have supported for the last hundred years the Strict Baptist Mission which maintains a small work in India, and amongst Tamil-speaking Indians elsewhere.

ANDREW FULLER AND EVANGELICAL CALVINISM

Though the influence of Isaac Watts and Philip Doddridge, as well as of such societies as the King's Head Society,[9] kept the majority of Congregationalists in the paths of Moderated or

A DEFINITION OF HYPER-CALVINISM 151

High Calvinism, many Particular Baptists adopted Hyper-Calvinism through the influence of Gill and Brine. Indeed, Hyper-Calvinism reigned supreme in many Churches until Andrew Fuller, minister of the Baptist Church in Kettering, where Gill and Brine had been nurtured, printed in 1785 his little book which helped to change the course of Baptist history. Its title was, *The Gospel Worthy of all Acceptation: or the Obligation of Men fully to credit and cordially to approve whatever God makes known. Wherein is considered, the Nature of Faith in Christ, and the Duty of those where the Gospel comes in that Matter.* In a letter to a friend in 1809, Fuller explained how he had come to the point where he had broken loose from the shackles of Hyper-Calvinism.

The principal writings with which I was first acquainted, were those of Bunyan, Gill and Brine. I had read pretty much of Dr. Gill's *Body of Divinity*, and from many parts of it had received considerable instruction. I perceived, however, that the system of Bunyan was not the same with his; for that while he maintained the doctrines of election and predestination, he nevertheless held with the free offer of salvation to sinners without distinction. These were things which I then could not reconcile, and therefore supposed that Bunyan, though a great and good man, was not so clear in his views of the doctrines of the Gospel as the writers who succeeded him. I found, indeed, the same things in all the old writers of the sixteenth and seventeenth centuries that came in my way. They all dealt, as Bunyan did, in free invitations to sinners to come to Christ and be saved; the consistency of which with personal election I could not understand. It is true, I perceived the Scriptures abounded with exhortations and invitations to sinners; but I supposed there must be two kinds of holiness, one of which was possessed by man in innocence, and was binding on all his posterity, the other derived from Christ, and binding only on his people. I had not yet learned that the same things which are required by the precepts of the law are bestowed by the grace of the gospel. Those exhortations to repentance and faith, therefore, which are addressed in the New Testament to the unconverted, I supposed refer only to such external repentance and faith, as were within their power, and might be complied with without the grace of God. The effect of these views was, that I had very little to say to the unconverted, at least nothing in a way of exhortation to things spiritually good, or certainly connected with salvation.

But in the autumn of 1775, being in London, I met with a pamphlet by Dr. Abraham Taylor, concerning what was called *The Modern Question*. I had never seen any thing relative to this controversy before, although the subject, as I have stated, had occupied my thoughts. I was but little impressed by his reasonings, till he came to the addresses of John the Baptist, Christ, and the Apostles which he proved to be addressed to the ungodly, and to mean spiritual repentance and faith, inasmuch as they were connected with the remission of sins. This set me fast. I read and examined the scripture passages, and the more I read and thought, the more I doubted of the justice of my former views.[10]

So in 1785 he wrote *The Gospel Worthy of All Acceptation*. The simple truths of this book soon penetrated the hearts and minds of many ministers and laymen, and alerted them to the need for the evangelisation of the world. At Kettering on the 2nd October, 1792, in the home of Mrs. Beeby Wallis, the widow of the great-grandson of the first minister of the Little Meeting, William Wallis, the Baptist Missionary Society was formed. Soon after William Carey sailed to India. From this time the greater part of the Particular Baptist denomination turned its back on Hyper-Calvinism.[11]

[1] Examples of practical antinomianism can be found amongst those who had adopted a Crispian-type theology. David Crossley, the predecessor of John Skepp in London, was excommunicated for drunkenness, immodest behaviour towards women, and an attempt to cover up his offences by the telling of lies. The story is told in "A faithful narrative of the proceedings of severall Brethren, and of this Church of Jesus Christ against Mr. David Crossley, their late pastor, from the beginning of december 1707 to the 14 of August 1709", "Minutes of the Particular Baptist church meeting in Curriers'-Hall", folios 32-36. (The Churchbook is in the Angus Library, Regent's Park College, Oxford.) Similar lapses, however, have been known from time to time among adherents of other theologies also!

[2] *A Defense of some important doctrines*, Vol. I, pp. 162 ff.

[3] *Ibid*, Vol. I, pp. 453 ff., and Vol. II, pp. 216 ff.

[4] *Ibid*, Vol. I, p. 48.

[5] The educated High Calvinists included men like Thomas Bradbury, Robert Bragge, Abraham Taylor, etc.

[6] Cf. P. Toon, "The Growth of a Supralapsarian Christology", *E.Q.* XXXIX (January, 1967), and "English Strict Baptists", *B.Q.* XXI (January, 1965).

[7] Quoted by Whitley, *Calvinism and Evangelism in England*, p. 28.

[8] *Ibid*, p. 28.

[9] See Appendix II.

[10] J. Ryland, *The Life and Death of the Reverend Andrew Fuller*, pp. 58 ff. (This John Ryland was the son of the John Ryland referred to above.)

[11] The best study of "Particular Baptist History, 1760-1820" is to be found in the Oxford D.Phil. Thesis (1965) by Olin Robison.

APPENDIX I

THE DIARY OF JOSEPH HUSSEY

Hussey's Diary is not a "diary" in the true sense of the word. It is in fact a form of note book in which Hussey recorded in chronological order incidental things pertaining to his ministry. Thus there are references to services he took, Biblical texts he used and to church meetings. On the flyleaf Hussey wrote:

> A Church-Book kept for my own Private Use, to register many Incidental Things: and especially my Preaching, Baptizing, and administring the Lord's Supper: together with a Register of the Names of my Pastoral Flock in Cambridge, from the year 1691, when they first called me to office, and on to the year 1719, written with my own Hand and attested by Me, Joseph Hussey.

In fact it also contains references to his ministry before 1691 and after 1719.

The book contains about five hundred pages, three-quarters of which deal with the years in Cambridge. It is bound in pig-skin and is approximately 7 in. × 8 in. × 1 in. Originally it included a Baptismal Register but this was ripped out in 1837 when the Government ordered all Nonconformist Registers to be deposited at Somerset House, London.

It is kept in the safe at Emmanuel Congregational Church, Cambridge, along with other valuable possessions of the Church. Since it is regarded as a proud possession, the Church has no immediate plans to lodge it in the Public Record Office.

The only study of the Diary which has been published is that by A. G. Matthews, *Diary of a Cambridge Minister* (1937), which was written to commemorate the two hundred and fiftieth anniversary of the founding of the Church. Mr. A. Smith, a deacon of the Church at the present time, has made a study of the Diary in recent days but has not yet published anything as a result of his research.

APPENDIX II

THE DOCTRINAL BASIS OF THE KING'S HEAD SOCIETY

Once each fortnight a group of ministers and laymen, some of whom had been connected with the Lime Street Lectures, met in the King's Head Tavern, Sweeting's Alley, near the Royal Exchange. They were Congregationalists and maintained an Academy in Deptford (later in Stepney), the first tutor being Abraham Taylor, one of the Lime Street lecturers. At the front of their Minute Books (now in New College, London) there is a "Declaration as to some controverted points of Christian Doctrine". After a short introduction ten points of doctrine are given.

Some Ministers and Gentlemen, being sensible of the great opposition, which has been of late to the Christian religion, agreed to use their utmost endeavours, to support the ancient and true Protestant doctrines: and as there are some points which are not controverted at present, they judged it proper to give a very brief summary of those doctrinal truths, which are now attack'd with the greatest vehemence, and which they had a special regard to, in the following articles.

I

The light of nature affords men so much knowledge as to the being and perfections of God, that they are without excuse, when they glorify him not as God; but it is not sufficient to give a saving knowledge of the Most High; therefore God was pleas'd to give a clear and full manifestation of his mind and will in the Scriptures of the old and new testament; which are the only and the perfect rule of faith and practice: and no doctrines are to be regarded, which are not there express'd, or deduced from there by necessary consequence. In the Scriptures nothing is reveal'd contrary to right reason; but many mysteries are there revealed, which transcend finite reason: and they are to be received on the authority of the revealer, without enquiring into the mode of them.

II

The light of nature informs us that there is but one God, and, that he is clothed with all possible perfections, and that besides one God, there can be no other. This doctrine of the unity of God is abundantly con-

THE DOCTRINAL BASIS OF THE KING'S HEAD SOCIETY

firm'd in the Scripture; but there it is reveal'd that in the unity of the Godhead, there are three persons, the Father, the Son, and the Holy Spirit, who are the same in nature, and all divine perfections; so that these three are the one supreme God, the one object of our faith and worship.

III

God, from eternity, unchangeably ordain'd whatsoever comes to pass, yet so, as that he is not the author of sin, nor is violence offer'd to the will of the creature; though he unchangeably knows whatsoever will come to pass yet he has not decreed anything, because he foresaw it would come to pass, on certain conditions. By his decree some of mankind are predestinated to everlasting life. These God, according to the good pleasure of his will, has chose in Christ, out of his meer sovereignty, without any foresight of faith or good works, as causes or conditions moving them thereto. Such whom he chose in Christ he chose that they might, in time, be holy and blameless before him; the rest of mankind, he, in his sovereign pleasure, has left to feel the consequence of their transgressions.

IV

God created our first parents in honour and innocence, and entered into a covenant of works with Adam, and all his posterity; but he broke this covenant by sinning against God. By this apostasy, he and we in him, fell from original righteousness, lost communication with God and so became dead in sin. The guilt of Adam's first sin is imputed to his posterity, and a corrupt nature is derived to them, whereby they are averse to all good, prone to all evil.

V

God the Father was pleased, before the foundation of the world, to enter in a covenant with Christ, the second Adam, and with all the elect in him, as his spiritual seed; in which agreement Christ undertook to do the work of a surety, in fulfilling the law, and suffering death, that he might bring his sons and daughters to glory. In this covenant, the most ample provision is made for the chosen people, so that all the blessings, pertaining to salvation are bestowed freely, and do not depend on any conditions, to be performed by the creature. In this God the Father show'd the greatness of his wisdom, in contriving a way, wherein, securing the rights of his justice, by punishing sin, in the person of the surety, he might yet show forth the riches of his grace, in saving sinners.

VI

When the fulness of time was come, God the Son, the surety of his people, and the mediator between God and them, took upon him the human nature, consisting of a true body, and a reasonable soul, not a super angelick spirit; which human nature he took into union with his divine person; so that Christ is truly God, and truly man in one person; he being made of a woman, was made under the law, and perfectly fulfilled it, by obeying its precepts and suffering the punishment due to us: he endured grievous torments in his soul, as well as pain in his body, and offering himself up in his human nature, which had an infinite value put upon it, arising from the union of that nature with his divine person, he yielded to the justice of God, a full and proper satisfaction for the sins of his people; by which he delivers from condemnation and gives a right to all spiritual blessings, and to the glory of heaven: the saving benefits of his death are extended no farther than to the elect, for whom he undertook, and in whose place he died: so as all are saved for whom Christ died, otherwise he must be supposed to have died in vain; and as all men are not actually saved, it follows, that he did not die for all men, or merely to put into a salvable state, all who will attempt to work out their own salvation, by improving upon the common helps that are afforded them.

VII

All that are saved, are justified by the righteousness of Christ, imputed to them. God pardons their sins and accepts them as righteous, not on account of any thing in them, but for Christ's sake alone; not by imputing faith itself, the act of believing, or sincere obedience, as their righteousness, but by imputing Christ's active and passive obedience, as their sole justifying righteousness. Though they receive Christ, and rest on him, and his merits by faith; yet that faith is not from themselves but is the Holy Spirit's work, and though, by that we receive the righteousness of Christ, yet it is not the condition, for the sake of which sinners are justified.

VIII

By the fall men have lost all ability of will for what is good and cannot by their own strength convert themselves, or prepare themselves for conversion, when they are effectually called; it is by the irresistible power and efficacy of the Holy Spirit, in which they are altogether passive and are quicken'd and enabled by him, to answer the call, to repent of their sins, to abound in good works, and to make a progress in holiness; which, though it is not the cause, or condition of salvation, yet it is a necessary part of it, and must be found, in all who hope to see the Lord with comfort.

IX

They who are sanctified, though they frequently sin, and so provoke God, as an offended Father, to chastise them, yet being kept by the power of the Holy Spirit, they will be recovered from their backslidings, and shall neither totally, nor finally fall from grace, but shall certainly persevere to the end.

X

After death, the souls of believers shall be perfectly holy and shall immediately pass into glory, and shall not sleep with their bodies, which are to be committed to the grave, till the last day: at which time, the same numerical bodies shall be raised from the dust of the earth in glory and honour, and shall be reunited to their souls, that in soul and body the saints may be for ever perfect with the Lord, and may keep up uninterrupted fellowship with the Father, Son and Holy Spirit, in the happy regions of rest and peace.

To the Father, to the Son, and to the Holy Spirit, three divine persons, and the one supreme God, be all honour and glory ascrib'd, now, henceforth, and for evermore. Amen.

BIBLIOGRAPHY
(The place of publication is London except where stated.)

I. PRIMARY SOURCES

(a) SELECT WORKS.

An Account of the Doctrine and Discipline of Mr. Richard Davis, 1700.
Ames, W., *The Marrow of Sacred Divinity*, 1642.
Arminius, J., *The Writings* (tr. J. Nichols and W. R. Bagnall), 3 vols., Grand Rapids, 1956.
Baxter, R., *The Scripture-Gospel Defended*, 1690.
Beart, J., *A Vindication of the Eternal Law and the Everlasting Gospel*, 1707.
Bentley, W., *The Lord the Helper of His People*, 1733.
Beza, Th., *Tractationes Theologiae*, 3 vols., Geneva, 1570-82.
Brine, J., *Ancient Prophecy proved to be Divine*, 1761.
— *An Antidote against a spreading Antinomian Principle*, 1750.
— *The Certain Efficacy of the Death of Christ asserted*, 1743.
— *Christ, the Object of God's Eternal Delight*, 1761.
— *The Christian Religion not destitute of arguments sufficient to support it*, 1743.
— *A Defence of the Doctrine of Eternal Justification*, 1732.
— *The Doctrines of the Imputation of Sin to Christ, and the Imputation of His Righteousness to His People*, 1757.
— *Motives to Love and Unity among Calvinists, who differ in some points*, 1753.
— *The Proper Eternity of the Divine Decrees*, 1754.
— *A Refutation of Arminian Principles, delivered in a pamphlet, intitled, The Modern Question*, 1743.
— *Remarks upon a Pamphlet intitled, Some doctrines in the superlapsarian scheme . . .*, 1736.
— *A Treatise on Various Subjects* (ed. James Upton), 1813.
— *A Vindication of some Truths of Natural and Revealed Religion*, 1746.
Calamy, E., *An Historical Account of My Own Life* (ed. J. T. Rutt), 2 vols., 1829.

BIBLIOGRAPHY

Calvin, J., *Concerning the Eternal Predestination of God* (tr. J. K. S. Reid), 1961.
— *The Institutes of the Christian Religion* (tr. H. Beveridge), 1962.
Charnock, S., *Discourse on the Existence and Attributes of God*, 1682.
Chauncy, I., *Neonomianism Unmask'd, or the Ancient Gospel Pleaded against the other called a New Law*, 2 vols., 1692-3.
— *The Doctrine which is according to Godliness*, 1694.
Cole, T., *A Discourse of Christian Religion*, 1692.
— *A Discourse of Regeneration, Faith and Repentance*, 1689.
— *The Incomprehensibleness of Imputed Righteousness*, 1692.
Crisp, T., *Christ Alone Exalted . . . being the Complete Works* (7th ed.), 1832.
Davis, R., *Hymns composed on several subjects* (7th ed., pref. by J. Gill), 1748.
— *Truth and Innocency Vindicated against falsehood*, 1692.
Declaration of the United Ministers against Mr. Richard Davis, 1692.
Declaration of the Congregational Ministers . . . against Antinomian Errours, 1699.
Defense of some Important Doctrines of the Gospel, 2 vols., 1732.
Edwards, J., *Crispianism Unmask'd, or a Discovery of . . . Erroneous Assertions in Dr. Crisp's Sermons*, 1693.
Edwards, T., *A Short Review of . . . "Crispianism Unmasked"*, 1693.
Firmin, G., *A Brief Review of Mr. Davis's Vindication*, 1693.
Fuller, A., *The Complete Works . . . with a memoir by Andrew G. Fuller*, 5 vols., 1831.
— *The Gospel Worthy of All Acceptation*, 1785.
Gill, J., *An Answer to the Birmingham Dialogue-Writer*, 1737. in *Sermons and Tracts*, Vol. II, 1773.
— *A Body of Doctrinal Divinity* (second edition), 3 vols., 1796.
— *The Cause of God and Truth* (new edition), 1855.
— *The Doctrine of God's Everlasting Love to His Elect and their Eternal Union with Christ*, 1732, in *Sermons and Tracts*, Vol. III, 1778.

Gill. J., *The Doctrine of Justification by the Righteousness of Christ, Stated and Vindicated*, 1730, in *Sermons and Tracts*, Vol. III.
— *The Doctrine of Predestination Stated, and set in Scripture-Light*, 1752, in *Sermons and Tracts*, Vol. III.
— *The Doctrine of the Saints' Final Perseverance Asserted and Vindicated*, 1752, in *Sermons and Tracts*, Vol. III.
— *The Doctrine of the Trinity Stated and Vindicated*, 1731, in *Sermons and Tracts*, Vol. III.
— *Exposition of the New Testament*, 3 vols., 1809.
— *Exposition of the Old Testament*, 6 vols., 1810.
— *The Law Established by the Gospel*, 1756, in *Sermons and Tracts*, Vol. I, 1773.
— *The Moral Nature and Fitness of Things Considered*, 1743, in *Sermons and Tracts*, Vol. II.
— *The Necessity of Good Works unto Salvation considered*, 1739, in *Sermons and Tracts*, Vol. II.
— *Truth Defended* (against Job Burt), 1736, in *Sermons and Tracts*, Vol. II.
Glass, N., *The Early History of the Independent Church at Rothwell*, Northampton, 1871.
Goodwin, T., *Exposition of Ephesians I*, in *Works* (ed. J. C. Miller), Vol. I, Edinburgh, 1862.
— *Of the Creatures*, in *Works*, Vol. VII.
— *Of the Knowledge of God the Father* . . ., in *Works*, Vol. IV.
Goodwin, T. (Jnr.), *A Discourse of the True Nature of the Gospel*, 1695.
Heppe, H., *Reformed Dogmatics* (tr. G. T. Thompson), 1950.
Hussey, J., *The Gospel-Feast Opened*, 1693.
— *The Glory of Christ Unveil'd or the Excellency of Christ Vindicated*, 1706.
— *God's Operations of Grace but No Offers of His Grace* (third edition), 1792.
Keach, B., *The Marrow of True Justification*, 1692.
Locke, J., *Essay Concerning Human Understanding* (ed. A. S. Pringle-Pattison), Oxford, 1960.
— *The Reasonableness of Christianity* (ed. I. T. Ramsey), 1958.

Lorimer, W., *An Apology for the Ministers who subscribed only unto the stating of the Truths and Errours in Mr. Williams' Book*, 1694.
— *Remarks on . . . Mr. Goodwin's Discourse of the Gospel*, 1696.
Mather, N., *The Righteousness of God through Faith*, 1694.
Matthews, A. G., *Diary of a Cambridge Minister*, Cambridge, 1937.
Maurice, M., *Monuments of Mercy*, 1729.
Owen, J., *The Death of Death in the Death of Christ* (new edition), 1959.
Pemble, W., *Vindiciae Gratiae*, 1627.
Perkins, W., *Works*, 3 vols., 1612.
Rehakosht, P. (John King), *A Plain and Just Account of a most horrid and dismal Plague begun at Rowel, alias Rothwell*, 1692.
Ridgley, T., *A Body of Divinity*, 2 vols., 1731-3.
Rippon, J., *A Brief Memoir of the Life and Writings of . . . John Gill*, 1838.
Ryland, J., *The Life and Death of Andrew Fuller*, 1816.
Skepp, J., *Divine Energy or the Efficacious Operations of the Spirit of God upon the soul of man* (third edition), 1851.
Stevens, J., *A Scriptural Display of the Triune God and the early existence of Jesus' human soul*, 1813.
Stockell, S., *The Redeemer's Glory Unveil'd*, 1733.
Torrance, T. F., *The School of Faith . . . Catechisms of the Reformation*, 1959.
Traill, R., *A Vindication of the Protestant Doctrine concerning Justification*, 1692, in *Works of Robert Traill*, Vol. I, Edinburgh, 1810.
Twisse, W., *Vindiciae Gratiae*, Amsterdam, 1632.
Watts, I., *The Glory of Christ as God-Man displayed*, 1746.
Watson, T., *A Body of Divinity* (new edition), 1965.
Wayman, L., *A Further Enquiry after Truth, wherein is shown what faith is required of unregenerate persons*, 1738.
— *Defence of A Further Enquiry after Truth*, 1739.
Williams, D., *Gospel-Truth Stated and Vindicated*, 1692.
— *Man made Righteous by Christ's Obedience*, 1694.

Wilson, W., *The History and Antiquities of Dissenting Churches and Meeting Houses in London, Westminster and Southwark*, 4 vols., 1808-10.

Witsius, H., *Conciliatory or Irenical Animadversions on the Controversies agitated in Britain under the unhappy names of Antinomians and Neonomians* (trans. T. Bell), Glasgow, 1807. Original Latin, Utrecht, 1696.

Zanchius, J., *The Doctrine of Absolute Predestination* (trans. A. Toplady), 1825.

(*b*) UNPUBLISHED MANUSCRIPTS.

Hussey, J., "Diary" (in the possession of Emmanuel Congregational Church, Cambridge).

"First Church Book of *Kimbolton* Independent Church" (typescript by H. G. Tibbutt in Dr. Williams's Library).

"Minutes of the Church meeting at the Bagnio, Newgate Street, and later at Curriers Hall, Cripplegate, 1691-1722" (in the possession of Regent's Park College, Oxford).

"Minutes of the King's Head Society" (in the possession of New College, London).

Rix, J., "The Nonconformist Churches at Hail-Weston, St. Neots, etc." (in the possession of Dr. Williams's Library).

II. SECONDARY SOURCES

(*a*) GENERAL WORKS OF REFERENCE.

Dictionary of Doctrinal and Historical Theology (ed. J. H. Blunt), 1871.

Dictionary of National Biography (ed. L. Stephen and S. Lee), 1937-8.

Encyclopaedia of Religion and Ethics (ed. J. Hastings), 1908-26.

The New Schaff-Herzog Encyclopedia of Religious Knowledge (ed. S. M. Jackson), 1908-12.

(*b*) SELECT WORKS.

Adams, H., *View of Religions*, 1814.

Berkhof, L., *Systematic Theology*, 1949.

BIBLIOGRAPHY

Boehl, E., *The Reformed Doctrine of Justification* (tr. C. H. Riedesel), Grand Rapids, 1946.
Boettner, L., *The Reformed Doctrine of Predestination*, Philadelphia, 1963.
Buchanan, J., *The Doctrine of Justification*, Edinburgh, 1867.
Carruthers, S. W., *The Everyday Work of the Westminster Assembly*, Philadelphia, 1943.
Clark, H. W., *History of English Nonconformity*, Vol. II, 1913.
Coleman, T., *Memorials of the Independent Churches in Northamptonshire*, 1853.
Colligan, J. H., *The Arian Movement in England*, Manchester, 1913.
Coomer, D., *English Dissent under the Early Hanoverians*, 1946.
Cragg, G. R., *From Puritanism to the Age of Reason*, Cambridge, 1950.
— *Reason and Authority in the Eighteenth Century*, Cambridge, 1964.
Dakin, A., *Calvinism*, 1940.
Dale, R. W., *History of English Congregationalism* (ed. A. W. W. Dale), 1907.
Davis, A. P., *Isaac Watts: His life and work*, 1948.
Dillenberger, J., *Protestant Thought and Natural Science*, 1961.
Dorner, J. A., *History of Protestant Theology*, Vol. I, Edinburgh, 1871.
Dowey, E. A., *The Knowledge of God in Calvin's Theology*, New York, 1952.
Duffield, G. E. (ed.), *John Calvin*, Abingdon, 1966.
Evans, J., *Sketch of the Denominations of the Christian World*, 1795.
Franks, R. S., *History of the Doctrine of the Work of Christ*, 2 vols., 1918.
Gordon, A., *Freedom After Ejection*, Manchester, 1917.
Griffiths, O. M., *Religion and Learning*, Cambridge, 1935.
Haller, W., *The Rise of Puritanism*, New York, 1938.
Hanson, L., *Government and the Press*, 1936.
Harrison, A. W., *The Beginnings of Arminianism to the Synod of Dort*, 1926.

Hastie, W., *The Theology of the Reformed Church in its fundamental principles*, Edinburgh, 1904.
Hodge, A. A., *The Confession of Faith* (new edition), 1958.
Hodge, C., *Systematic Theology*, 3 vols., Grand Rapids, 1953.
Howell, W. S., *Logic and Rhetoric in England, 1500-1700*, Princeton, 1956.
Huehns, G., *Antinomianism in English History*, 1951.
Jansen, J. F., *Calvin's Doctrine of the Work of Christ*, 1956.
Jones, J. A. (ed.), *Bunhill Memorials*, 1849.
Jones, R. Tudur, *Congregationalism in England, 1662-1962*, 1962.
de Jong, A. C., *The Well-Meant Gospel Offer*, Franeker, n.d.
Kelly, J. N. D., *Early Christian Doctrines*, 1960.
Kevan, E. F., *The Grace of Law*, 1964.
Kneale, W. & M., *The Development of Logic*, 1962.
Laplanche, F., *Orthodoxie et Prédication: Loeuvre d'Amyraut*, Paris, 1965.
McLachlan, H., *English Education under the Test Acts*, Manchester, 1931.
McLachlan, H. J., *Socinianism in Seventeenth Century England*, 1951.
MacLeod, J., *Scottish Theology*, Edinburgh, 1943.
McNeill, J. T., *The History and Character of Calvinism*, New York, 1954.
Marsden, J. B., *History of the Later Puritans*, 1852.
Marshall, D., *Eighteenth Century England*, 1962.
Matthews, A. G. (ed.), *The Savoy Declaration of Faith and Order, 1658*, 1959.
Miller, P., *Errand into the Wilderness*, Cambridge, Mass., 1956.
— *The New England Mind: The Seventeenth Century*, Cambridge, Mass, 1954.
More, L. T., *Isaac Newton*, New York, 1934.
Murray, J. (with N. B. Stonehouse), *The Free Offer of the Gospel*, Phillipsburg, New Jersey, 1948.
— *Calvin on Scripture and Divine Sovereignty*, Grand Rapids, 1960.
Neve, J. L., *A History of Christian Thought*, 2 vols., Philadelphia, 1946.

Nuttall, G. F. (with R. Thomas, H. L. Short and R. D. Whitehorn), *Beginnings of Nonconformity* (The Hibbert Lectures), 1964.
Nuttall, G. F., *The Holy Spirit in Puritan Faith and Experience*, Oxford, 1946.
— (ed.), *Philip Doddridge*, 1951.
— *Richard Baxter*, 1965.
Nutter, B., *The Story of the Cambridge Baptists*, 1912.
Ong, W. J., *Ramus. Method and Decay of Dialogue*, Cambridge, Mass., 1958.
Paul, S. F., *Historical Sketch of the Gospel Standard Baptists*, 1945.
Payne, E. A., *College Street, Northampton, 1697-1947*, 1947.
Porter, H. C., *Reformation and Reaction in Tudor Cambridge*, 1958.
Powicke, F. J., *The Cambridge Platonists*, 1926.
Rex, W., *Essays on Pierre Bayle and Religious Controversy*, The Hague, 1965.
Ritschl, A., *A Critical History of the Christian Doctrine of Justification and Reconciliation* (tr. J. S. Black), Edinburgh, 1872.
Rogers, A. K., *A Student's History of Philosophy*, New York, 1962.
Rogers, J. B., *Scripture in the Westminster Confession*, Kampen, 1966.
Schaff, P., *The Creeds of the Evangelical Protestant Churches*, 1877.
Schmidt, A. M., *Calvin and the Calvinistic Tradition*, 1960.
Schrenk, G., *Gottesreich und Bund in älteren Protestantismus*, Gütersloh, 1928.
Seeberg, R., *The History of Doctrines*, 2 vols., Grand Rapids, 1956.
Shirren, A. J., *The Chronicles of the Fleetwood House*, 1951.
Smith, J. W. A., *The Birth of Modern Education*, 1955.
Smith, N. K., *John Locke*, Manchester, 1933.
Steele, D. N. (with C. C. Thomas), *The Five Points of Calvinism*, Philadelphia, 1963.

Stoughton, J., *Religion in England under Queen Anne and the Georges*, Vol. I, 1878.
Stromberg, R. N., *Religious Liberalism in Eighteenth Century England*, 1954.
Thomas, R., *Daniel Williams: Presbyterian Bishop*, 1964.
Toulmin, J., *Historical View of the State of the Protestant Dissenters in England*, 1814.
Tulloch, J., *Rational Theology and Christian Philosophy in England in the Seventeenth Century*, 2 vols., 1872.
Wallace, R. S., *Calvin's Doctrine of the Christian Life*, Edinburgh, 1959.
Warfield, B. B., *Calvin and Augustine*, Philadelphia, 1956.
Whiting, C. E., *Studies in English Puritanism, 1660-1688*, 1931.
Whitley, W. T., *A History of British Baptists*, 1923.
— *Calvinism and Evangelism in England especially among Baptists*, n.d.
Wilkinson, J. T., *1662 and After: Three Centuries of English Nonconformity*, 1962.
Willey, B., *The Eighteenth Century Background*, 1940.
Wood, T., *English Casuistical Divinity during the Seventeenth Century*, 1952.
Yolton, J. W., *John Locke and the Way of Ideas*, 1956.

(c) ARTICLES.

Bangs, C., "Arminius and the Reformation", *C.H.* XXX (1961).
Crippen, T. G., "The Ancient Merchants' Lecture", *T.C.H.S.* VII (1916-18).
Davidson, N., "The Westminster Confession of Faith", *Scottish Journal of Theology*, XIX, No. 3 (1966).
Emerson, E. H., "Calvin and Covenant Theology", *C.H.* XXV (1956).
Henderson, G. D., "The Idea of Covenant in Scotland", *E.Q.* XXVII (1955).
Lindsay, T. M., "Covenant Theology", *British and Foreign Evangelical Review*, XXVIII (1879).
Møller, J. G., "The Beginnings of Puritan Covenant Theology", *J.E.H.* XIV (1963).

Nuttall, G. F., "Northamptonshire and 'The Modern Question': A Turning-Point in Eighteenth Century Dissent", *J.Th.S.* XVI (1965).
Parker, T. H. L., "Calvin's Doctrine of Justification", *E.Q.* XXIV (1952).
Solt, L. F., "John Saltmarsh. New Model Army Chaplain", *J.E.H.* II (1951).
Sprunger, K. L., "Ames, Ramus, and the Method of Puritan Theology", *Harvard Theological Review*, LIX (1966).
Thomas, R., "The Non-Subscription Controversy amongst Dissenters in 1719", *J.E.H.* IV (1953).
Toon, P., "English Strict Baptists", *B.Q.* XXI (1965).
— "The Growth of a Supralapsarian Christology", *E.Q.* XXIX (1967).
Von Rohr, J., "Covenant and Assurance in Early English Puritanism", *C.H.* XXXIV (1965).
White, B. R., "Thomas Crosby, Baptist Historian", *B.Q.* XXI (1965).
— "John Gill in London, 1719-1729", *B.Q.* XXII (1967).
Whitebrook, J. C., "The Life and Works of Mrs. Ann Dutton", *Transactions Baptist Historical Society*, VII (1920-1).

(*d*) UNPUBLISHED THESES

Breward, I., "The Life and Theology of William Perkins, 1558-1602", Ph.D., Manchester, 1963.
Bruggink, D. J., "The Theology of Thomas Boston, 1676-1732", Ph.D., Edinburgh, 1956.
Clipsham, E. F., "Andrew Fuller's Doctrine of Salvation", B.D., Oxford, 1965.
Kirkby, A. H., "The Theology of Andrew Fuller and its relation to Calvinism", Ph.D., Edinburgh, 1956.
Packer, J. I., "The Redemption and Restoration of Man in the thought of Richard Baxter", D.Phil., Oxford, 1954.
Pytches, P. N. L., "A Critical Exposition of the teaching of John Owen on the work of the Holy Spirit in the individual", M.Litt., Bristol, 1966-7.

Robison, O., "Particular Baptist History, 1760-1820", D.Phil., Oxford, 1965.
Seymour, R. E., "John Gill. Baptist Theologian, 1697-1771", Ph.D., Edinburgh, 1954.
Spears, W. E., "The Baptist Movement in England in the late Seventeenth Century as reflected in the work and thought of Benjamin Keach, 1640-1704", Ph.D., Edinburgh, 1953.

INDEX

ALLEN, J., 149
Alsop, V., 53, 66
Alsted, J. H., 24-5
Altingius, J., 99
Ames, W., 21, 24, 25, 60, 65, 68, 100, 143-4
Amyraut, M., 22, 73
Aquinas, T., 13, 73
Arius, 73
Arminius, J., 18 ff., 24, 73, 133
Athanasius, 73
Augustine (of Hippo), 11, 73, 88, 99

BAILEY, R., 96
Ball, J., 23
Bangs, C., 18
Bates, W., 67
Baxter, R., 22-3, 28, 40, 50 ff., 70, 112
Beart, J., 84
Becker, C. L., 104
Benson, G., 39
Bentley, W., 85, 148
Berkeley, G., 34
Beverley, T., 53
Beza, T., 13 ff., 24, 26, 73, 75, 127
Billio, R., 72
Blondel, D., 22
Bourn, S., 39
Bradbury, T., 45, 131, 138
Bragge, R., 43, 45, 111, 145
Bradwardine, T., 73
Breward, I., 15
Brine, J., 45, 94 ff., 105 ff., 119 ff., 144 ff.
Bruggink, D. J., 30
Bucer, M., 11
Bullinger, H., 12, 21
Bunyan, J., 151
Bures, R., 66
Burt, J., 98
Butler, J., 34

CALAMY, E., 40
Calvin, J., 11 ff., 39, 73, 82-3, 115 ff., 127 ff., 130, 143-4
Cameron, J., 22
Cappel, L., 22

Carey, W., 150-2
Chauncy, I., 53 ff.
Christian, F., 12
Clark, S., 41, 53
Clarke, S., 37 ff.
Clavier, H., 116
Clement, 73
Cocceius, J., 99, 103
Cokayn, G., 66
Cole, T., 51 ff., 82
Colligan, J. H., 45, 138
Collins, A., 35
Collins, J., 67
Coomer, D., 44
Coward, W., 42
Cragg, G. R., 45
Crippen, T. G., 67
Crisp, S., 49 ff.
Crisp, T., 28, 30, 49 ff., 82-3, 96 ff., 145
Crossley, D., 152
Cudworth, H., 32
Culverwell, N., 23
Cunningham, W., 15

DAILLÉ, J., 22
Davenant, Bishop, 23
Davis, J., 97, 102
Davis, R., 51 ff., 70, 73, 93 ff., 131
Dickson, D., 21
Dillenberger, J., 29
Doddridge, P., 40 ff., 150
Dodwell, H., 35, 103
Downame, G., 24
Duplessis-Mornay, 22
Dutton, A., 88, 149
Dutton, B., 135

EATON, J., 28, 30, 145
Edwards, J., 53
Edwards, T., 53, 67
Emerson, E. H., 30

FIRMIN, G., 67
Firmin, T., 36
Flavell, J., 30, 50
Fleming, R., 45
Foster, J., 39

Fowler, E., 45
Fuller, A., 144 ff.

GAMMON, J., 66
Gill, J., 45, 96 ff., 105 ff., 119 ff., 144 ff.
Gill, E., 97
Glass, N., 67, 102
Gomarus, F., 21, 74
Goodwin, P., 45
Goodwin, T. (Snr.), 25, 65, 76 ff., 88, 96, 100, 101, 134 ff.
Goodwin, T. (Jnr.), 53, 66, 138
Gordon, A., 67
Griffith, G., 66, 68
Griffiths, O. M., 45

HALL, B., 18
Hall, T., 45
Hallet, J., 37-8
Harrison, A. W., 29
Hartley, D., 32
Heideggerus, J. H., 99
Hemmingius, N., 16
Henderson, G. D., 29
Heppe, H., 30, 117, 138
Hodge, C., 20
Hoornbeck, J., 99, 116
Howe, J., 50, 53, 66
Huehns, G., 30
Hume, D., 34
Humfrey, J., 53, 67
Hurrion, J., 45, 145
Hussey, J., 26, 43, 66, 70 ff., 96 ff., 107, 144 ff.
Hutcheson, F., 40

ILLYRICUS, F., 16
Inge, W. R., 45

JACKSON, A., 131, 138
Jenkyn, W., 67
Jennings, J., 41

KEACH, B., 53, 61
Keate, Sir J., 72
Kelly, J. N. D., 90
Kevan, E. F., 58
Keyser, J., 53, 67
King, J., 67, 72
Knollys, H., 66

LANCASTER, R., 28, 30
Lardner, N., 39
Law, W., 34
Lobb, S., 53, 68
Locke, J., 31 ff., 67, 86
Lombard, P., 73
Lorimer, W., 53-4, 67
Luther, M., 11, 17, 74

MACCOVIUS, J., 60, 74, 99, 133
Macgowan, J., 149
McLachlan, H., 45
McLachlan, H. J., 45
Manton, T., 67
Mather, I., 66
Mather, N., 51, 53, 61, 66
Matthews, A. G., 89, 153
Maurice, M., 131, 138
Mead, M., 68
Melanchthon, P., 11
Miller, P., 25
Milton, J., 33
Møller, J. C., 29
Moore, J., 100-1, 103
More, H., 32
More, L. T., 45
Morgan, T., 35
Morris, I., 103
Morton, C., 72
Murray, J., 29
Musculus, W., 21

NEGUS, E., 87
Nesbitt, J., 68
Nestorius, 73
Newton, I., 33 ff., 37
Newton, J., 150
Nuttall, G. F., 45, 139
Nutter, B., 103

OLEVIANUS, C., 21
Ong, W. J., 30
Owen, J., 67, 96, 100, 130, 134 ff., 143-4

PACKER, J. I., 30, 54-5
Payne, E. A., 103
Peirce, J., 37-8
Pemble, W., 64, 69, 100, 101, 143
Perkins, W., 13 ff., 21, 75, 143
Perry, J., 102

INDEX

Piscator, J., 24
Porter, H. C., 29, 44
Powell, T., 66
Powicke, F. J., 45
Preston, J., 23
Priestley, J., 40

RAMUS, P., 24, 68, 76 ff.
Rex, W., 22
Richardson, A., 24-5, 68
Ridgley, T., 43, 107
Rippon, J., 102-3
Ritschl, A., 29
Rix, J., 102
Rogers, J. B., 29
Rollock, R., 21
Rutherford, S., 21, 100, 138
Ryland, J., 152
Ryland, J. C., 100, 150

SALTMARSH, J., 28, 30, 145
Scandrett, S., 72
Schrenk, G., 30
Schweizer, A., 12
Skepp, J., 85 ff., 97 ff., 125, 144 ff.
Sladen, J., 45
Smith, J., 32
Smith, J. W. Ashley, 69
Smith, N. K., 45
Sozzini, F., 36, 74
Sprunger, K. L., 30
Spurgeon, C. H., 150
Stephens, L., 45
Stevens, J., 149
Stillingfleet, E., 33, 53
Stockell, S., 44, 46, 84-5, 108, 147-9
Stogden, H., 38
Stromberg, R. N., 35

TAYLOR, A., 43, 98, 131, 138, 145, 151, 154
Taylor, J., 39, 103, 138
Taylor, R., 67-8
Temple, W., 24
Thomas, R., 41, 66-7
Tibbutt, H. G., 102
Tillotson, J., 33
Tindal, M., 35

Toland, J., 35
Tomkins, M., 45
Toon, P., 46, 152
Toplady, A., 100
Traill, R., 53, 66
Trinterud, L. J., 30
Turner, J., 66
Twisse, W., 13, 64, 69, 75, 100, 110, 116, 138, 143
Tyndale, W., 21

URSINUS, Z., 21
Ussher, Archbishop, 23

VINES, R., 23
Von Rohr, J., 30

WALLACE, R. S., 138
Wallis, T., 97, 100
Wallis, W., 96, 152
Warfield, B., 20
Watson, T., 69
Watts, I., 40, 43, 103, 121, 129, 150
Wayman, L., 95 ff., 104 ff., 119 ff., 144 ff.
Wendel, F., 29, 118, 138
Wendelinus, M. F., 99
Wesley, J., 34, 52, 98, 129
Whateley, W., 23
Whichcote, B., 32
Whiston, W., 37, 103
Whitaker, R., 72, 89
Whitby, D., 98
White, B. R., 103
Whitefield, G., 150
Whitley, W. T., 139, 150
Williams, D., 40, 50 ff.
Wilson, S., 45, 145
Wilson, W., 89
Wing, D., 67
Witsius, H., 53, 67, 99, 101
Wollebius, J., 24, 99

YOLTON, J. W., 45
Young, S., 53, 67

ZWINGLI, U., 11, 21, 115